Why People Fight

Why People **Fight**

Ivanhoe Chaput

Table of Contents

Prologue.. 1

1: Are We Born To Fight?................................... 5

2: We Simply Can't Be Wrong 14

3: The Psychology Of Lying 19

4: Our Reaction To Annoyances Could Be Genetic 29

5: Disputes Over Change........................... 35

6: Why Tempers Flare 40

7: Animals Fight Too 47

8: Logic, Reasoning Visual And Audio Input 53

9: Revenge 61

10: Fighting The Good Fight........................ 67

11: Unprovoked Aggression........................ 73

12: Fighting Comes In Waves 77

13: Human Experience Is Only About Seventy Years...... 83

14: Those Fighting Youths....................... 90

15: We Come Here By Design.................. 97

16: Two Realities............................ 103

Most people are like a coin.

On one side is the word "Love," and on the other is the word "Hate."

Prologue

Writing this book has made a profound change in the way I view and run my life. When I was in my late teens, I was rebellious against any authority that tried to influence me, even if it was for my benefit. Teenage brains process input differently from adults. Teenagers' reward sensitivity that threads data together separate after they get into their twenties. The foundation for building adolescence is comprised of stages. These are roughly divided into ages eleven to fourteen, fifteen to seventeen and eighteen to twenty-one. But what was learned in those teenage years lingered throughout my life; change was slow, unless there was some jolt or impactful new information that altered what I had taken into my mental library.

Understanding why people fight was one of those profound changes.

From my research into why people fight, I've become more tolerant. I see people's, and my own, annoyances and disagreements over beliefs, ideas and perceptions as more of a passing journey than a reaction to a present situation. I've found myself to be more compassionate toward others with an understanding that their entrenched ideas are merely a product of external data, and that within all of us is a being looking, hearing and feeling the experience of life. Oh, I still get angry; I still have a bit of a temper, but it's overshadowed with knowledge as to why we fight and not that fighting will bring about some resolve—although certain provocation can only be resolved with physical action.

I'm not against fighting as a belief that fighting is bad. I'm also not for it where there's no purposeful reason behind some unprovoked aggression. The aggressor deserves their just desserts, just as 9/11 required a commensurate response. But this book is not about political or international fighting, although I do include studies on war in general. It's more about reasons for aggression that trigger people to fight. Personally, I don't like fighting unless it involves some bout where the winner and loser shake hands over a fight well fought. Fighting has been a demonstration of brawn and brain for millennia. In ancient cultures, it drew crowds paying to watch their favorite fighters either win or lose, sometimes to the death. In our present day, a broad spectrum of fighting is watched on television. We can sit back and watch a war being fought with Oliver North's *War Stories*, see bombs being dropped in the Middle East and see two guys inside an octagonal ring pound on each other until one submits or gets knocked out.

On our streets and in person, it's a different feeling altogether. Not everyone likes to fight and not everyone likes to watch people fight. But when it happens, it nearly always gathers a crowd in which some onlookers appear to immediately make a decision as to who they'd prefer to win, while others wish they would take their aggression out somewhere else. Taking sides is a human attribute and so is wishing it would stop. Ideally a good fight is where the nerd whoops the bully. A lone defender knocking out five or more attackers is always a crowd-pleaser. But what about when someone is attacked to have their money stolen, or attacked for no reason at all? What is it that causes little annoyances to escalate into an outright brawl in which someone gets really hurt or even killed? Why is it that our differences draw a line between different cultures, ideologies, politics, religion, race and even gender? What is hate?

Not all fighting is physical. Couples are said to have had a fight of words over kids or money. Political opponents will put up a good fight and the medical field fights cancer and other diseases. Hence it can be said that some fights are for good reasons. But in the end, all fighting creates disturbance.

Other than what we came into this world with through our DNA, my research about fighting coughed up less tangible substance as to the psychology behind it than physical anomalies of the brain. The majority of information revolves around the physiological aspects relating to brain circuits, brain activity and release of chemicals in the brain. Psychologically, most information relates to opponents psyching their opponent out prior to a fighting match. Mental preparation is actually as important, if not more important, than physical prowess. There is also lots of data on why humans wage war, but information as to the reasons typical fighting between people just getting pissed off with each other took more digging. That is, unless one looked up information on road rage, office conflicts with coworkers and people clobbering out their differences under the heading of street fighting— lots of street fighting. However, these didn't provide much on root reasons why people fight; only what they were fighting over.

Curiosity may have killed a cat or two, but fighting is a trait that for me has carved out a myriad of questions about living on terra firma. If you've read my previous books, you'll know that I essentially live in the question. Having gotten into a few fights and mostly verbal fighting, I wanted to learn what it is about being here in a physical reality that invokes the emotion of hate that subsequently turns into a fight. It was also very interesting to find out that little in the study of psychology has been documented concerning hate. References to love abound, but when it comes to hate, it's as if it is something you can catch like a virus and is simply avoided. Hate is a forerunner to a physical confrontation, and yet it's a subject that psychologists and researchers appear to have an aversion to. As I mentioned above, fortunately there were a few references where researchers have done brain scans to find things like hate circuits and what makes criminals hang onto hate longer than nonviolent people.

My wife is probably the least violent, most loving and caring person I've ever met. When I told her that I was thinking of writing a book on why people fight, she immediately became very interested. She's certainly not in a class of her own. In all cultures throughout history, fighting has been elevated to a spectator sport where combatants can exhibit their physical deftness. A good fighter has to be strong and possess mental expertise in exerting technique as well as strength. In sports, combatants refer to fighting each other as competition. Competition may be associated with learning from each other, but in fighting, especially when it's not within the area of sports, the greatest lesson we can learn is that winning brings about a feeling of reward and losing conjures up revenge. It's like a circular escalating pattern with no positive ending.

What causes our minds and thoughts to resort to fighting when all that existed in the initial spark was mere disagreement? What makes us go into a rage when someone either accidentally or even purposefully cuts us off with their four-wheeled metal protective box? Why did Billy the Kid go so far as to shoot someone for snoring loudly in the next room of his hotel? This incident might be a myth, but I'm sure someone has done something similar.

These questions and more will be addressed herein, so let's get into why people fight!

Are We Born To Fight?

What remains a question in my mind is how people in general can be so immersed in their mindsets that they will resort to violent acts to merely prove their points of view that they are correct and that anyone that disagrees with them are wrong.

It's like we're all tiny little gods with power over our domains.

I was driving down Hawthorne Boulevard this morning and thought of a book by Dennis Prager titled *Why We Fight*. I was always intrigued by the title and wanted to find out more about it. I went to my office and decided to look up what the internet had to say about the book. I was totally blown away about what came up; it wasn't anything I expected. I then went to YouTube to listen to Dennis Prager's video on the subject. What I heard was totally off my perception of what the title might have been all about. I agree with Mr. Prager about why we fought for our freedom during the Great War and World War II. I agree that we also need to continue to preserve the freedoms that this great country provides for everyone, even those that hate America and are still living here.

I must be so far outside the box of "normal" thinking that I had to reevaluate my own ideas about who I was in the mix of the human family by misunderstanding Dennis's title. I was so far off from what it was about. I actually thought that the question about why we fight had to do with how our brains work and how we pick up information about our surroundings that drive us into pigeonholes of personal preferences and differences. Once inside these holes, anything outside of these quirks of "being" tends to annoy us because they don't fit within our paradigms of how things should be. That's how far off base I was.

Rather than being a question of how our personal perceptions take each of us in different reactionary directions over similar circumstances and ideas, it was about defending our political or national freedom and perceptions over different political and national perceptions. In other words, it was about fighting over our preservation—war and fighting for what we as a nation believe in. I had to wrestle a bit over what I thought was so blatantly obvious. After I thought more about it, I was inspired to sit down and write what I *thought* the book might have been about. Thanks for the inspiration, Dennis.

We all have our own developed approaches to life's circumstances. A person may like the idea of pain associated with sex and another is turned off by any sort of pain. The tailgater may have no idea he's annoying the person ahead of him. Nikola Tesla couldn't stand women wearing earrings. I don't like people with no sense of humor.

Here's a made-up scenario that's probably happened at some point, since just about everything under the sun has. There's a guy in a restaurant eating his food with his mouth open, smacking and chomping his gums, annoying the girl sitting at a table across from him so much that she makes a terse comment about his eating habits. He then tells her to mind her own business. Her boyfriend sitting with her gets up, picks up the man's plate, and dumps it over his head. The sloppy eater pulls out a gun. Oops!

Since I made that one up, it might not have the personal interest that this actual event does. In jolly old England, about one hundred people were having a great time chatting in a pub. A couple of guys began arguing over the last bag of peanuts when one lamped the other.

(I think "lamped" means something like he cold-cocked the other guy, in American-style English.) Before anyone could say supercalafragalisticexpialadoshus, half the pub's patrons, fifty in all, had engaged in a raucous of lamping that spilled out into the street—a bout of chaos. The police were called and had to spray the brawlers with incapacitant, probably our equivalent of pepper spray. In America, we might wish to sue the peanut packer for damages for not providing enough bags for everyone.

On a macro scale, in a film by Eugene Jarecki, he illustrates how President Eisenhower viewed the United States as the greatest force for good on the planet. His film also shows war to be a huge profit generator for many corporations and creates millions of jobs. Senator John McCain stated that we have an obligation to spread democracy and freedom throughout the world. Conversely, with war, lives are lost and there is destruction of homes and families. Cities, and sometimes complete countries, must be rebuilt and governments reshaped in their aftermath. What is considered good for some may result in horrible circumstances for others.

This book in not about greed and conquest, although greed is a part of why we fight. Wars are generally fought over commodities and territories that can produce them—although other factors, such as power and glory, have influenced decision-makers to wage war. The anticipated gains must outweigh its incurred cost. In most cases, war begins when bargaining fails to bring satisfactory results. Unsatisfactory results are an offshoot of irrationality or poor judgment, but mostly from the rational view and strength of the opposing enemy. In simple terms, a country attacks to gain something they deem valuable; the attacked country retaliates with the help of a consortium of alleys, and the attacking country is leveled. All is fair in love and war.

Wars have been less often fought over religious beliefs, but that depends on what historical era one focuses on. It can also be associated with glory. Religious wars can fall outside the realm of rationality based on the motivations that leaders are acting on behalf of a higher power. Thus, religious wars can be viewed as having non-rational explanations. Beliefs govern motives for religious wars.

Aside from war, in my way of thinking, what's easy to understand are the different points of view when analyzing reasons and logic behind beliefs that lead to conflict. What remains a question in my mind is how people in general can be so immersed in their mindsets that they will resort to violent acts to merely prove their points of view that they are correct and that anyone that disagrees with them are wrong. There are aggressors and defenders of aggression, good guys and bad guys. Too often the good guys don't realize they are bad guys in the eyes of the bad guys that believe they are the good guys, and vice versa.

What makes this even more complex is the idea that there is a God that will defend the good guys—whichever side they're on. During World War II, it was Germans fighting Americans, but also Christians fighting Christians who prayed that God would protect them against their enemy—that other Christian. The Italians switched sides during that conflict. Although political reasons are cited in historical records, could it also be so they wouldn't lose face because the Pope lived there? What many people don't know is that Italy switched sides during World War I as well. I won't go into the political details, but I found this to be interesting from the idea that a collective subconscious or group-thought might have been at work.

War is the grandest scope of why people fight. After misunderstanding Dennis Prager's title for his book, I wanted to understand why fighting occurs on an individual, or much smaller, scale. Why did a guy I knew that had somewhat of a temper beat his neighbor so badly he required surgery on his face over a borrowed lawnmower? Why was there a disagreement that escalated into a fistfight between two coworkers I knew when they ran into each other outside a Bank of America? What prompted the high school bully to attack me for no apparent reason during an assembly where I had to defend myself by breaking his arm? (By the way, after that we became good friends.)

The reasons why we fight can become even more complex when deep-seated desires motivate our behavior and certain brain circuits activate the fight/flight instinct. We are in a physical world of stuff. There is a belief amongst us that stuff, things, money, that really special car or that dream house will bring happiness. Studies have shown that if we experience something that stimulates a certain pleasure center within our brains, our emotions respond in kind.

There's also a dark side of pleasure. That's when there's some adrenaline rush when certain personality types do harm and get a pleasurable thrill from it. The first part, the detectable pleasure place in the brain, is physiological. It's located in the amygdale, or prefrontal cortex that regulates emotions (note it "regulates" and does not create) and the nucleus accumbens that controls the release of dopamine. Other parts include the medial forebrain bundle and the thalamus. These centers are interconnected and innervate the hypothalamus that informs it of the presence of rewards. There is also a part of the brain that has what is called the punishment circuit. This is when acetylcholine is released, which stimulates the secretion of adrenocorticotropic hormone that in turn causes the adrenal gland to release adrenaline for fight-or-flight decisions. Stimulation of this circuit can inhibit the pleasure circuit that can, in turn, drive out many pleasures.

These are all biochemical reactions to situations. A secondary aspect of the thinking function, the origin of emotion and desire, are nowhere to be found in any of the studies I found on fighting or hate. This is the mind part of us that, to this day, doesn't appear to be anywhere in physical space. It's the mind/brain problem that has scientists and philosophers at odds. The scant studies of fighting and hate further intrigued me to assert that the mind, that part of us that's literally nowhere in space and doesn't show up on any instruments, must also be recognized as a source where these urges and emotions may originate. The hot and cold spots registered in brain scans might just be the result of mind activity and not the reason for origination of thought. This does not refer to the possible influence of DNA upon personality. In other words, it's my belief that we are not our brains, and I'm not the lone ranger in this arena.

Why do we fight? It would be easy to answer this question with, "Because we can." And that just might be the best answer. When science revealed that the earth was not at the center of the universe, there were more questions. We discovered that we are part of a galaxy of billions of stars, but again there were more questions. The Big Bang revealed that the universe came from a monumental explosion, and then again, there were even more questions. It was much simpler to just believe that in the beginning there was God and he simply made everything—no further questions.

To answer why we fight with the easy answer above might also be to say it's because it can invoke further inquiry. If we can, why is it that we can? What or who allows this ability to cause our brains to trigger circuits of disagreement, displeasure, then anger, and follow this up with a circuit of violent action, and then follow this up with the stimulation of some pleasure circuit? Yes, victory over our opponent or enemy is euphoric! Just observe the guy in the octagon right after he's knocked the crap out of his opponent. Go on YouTube and see video of the jubilation after Japan surrendered from two cities destroyed in literally a couple of flashes.

Check out street-fight knockouts on YouTube and observe the reaction of the crowd when some poor guy, or in some cases the bully, gets knocked out cold. I found the crowd's reactions more revealing than the reaction of the guy that knocked out the other guy. What piqued my interest was that in many cases, the person narrating the video would laugh when someone was knocked out. Others would shout an expletive like, "Holy shit!" Overall, the reaction was that of surprised excitement. Even though I'm not one that likes to fight, I was drawn into watching these. The more I watched them, the more I began to like watching them. I was more drawn to the "bully being laid out by some little guy" videos. The others I liked to watch were those in which robbers picked the wrong store clerk and things turned on them. If I'm somewhat typical, then, restitution must be something that's ingrained in most people's psychological base. I even thought of what it would feel like to punch an attacker and knock him out—give him what he deserved. Wouldn't that be a thrill? But I'm past the point of having enough strength to do anything of the sort. It would have to be in a next life.

I had lots of questions as to why we fight. Might we engage in potential conflict in order to reap the reward of having our pleasure centers exude dopamine into our brains like the high an addict gets from an injection of his preferred drug? Could it be that we believe in a reward from our god or God that some words written down thousands of years ago will provide us with ultimate pleasures if we fight the good fight? Are our differences in even the smallest of actions, like squeezing the toothpaste from the middle of the tube rather than from the end, cause for conflict and even violence—even the last bag of peanuts? Do we fight because it just might also be fun? Maybe it's all of the above and more.

I once got into a fight, and I will say I won the fight. In fact, I've done it a couple of times and fortunately, never received a whoopin'. I've also had near-fights where I felt like I actually won because I was able to out-talk and maybe out-think the guy that wanted to pound me into the ground. Each time, I felt my pleasure center giving me a rush of satisfaction. I also experienced a fear of what might have happened if things had not gone in my favor. The fear was never while trying to defend myself by clobbering the other guy or outsmarting him. It usually occurred right before going to sleep. I would think about how much I would be smarting right then. In the South, when we say, "Ow, that smarts," that means it really, really hurts! Its origin is very old, stemming from the word, "smerten," which rhymes with hurtin'.

This teeter-totter between a rush and whatever might have happened had the balance of power, so to speak, gone the other way is probably why I never started a fight in my life. I only finished a few—very few. You never know how things will turn out. I don't like or enjoy fighting, or even arguing. I'm very uncomfortable with confrontation. I studied martial arts for many years and enjoyed winning bouts with opponents in the dojo (classroom). I liked the part where we bowed to each other out of respect after a match. It was competition in which we learned from each other. Today, competition has taken on more of a "beat the daylights out of your opponent and then gloat about it" mentality.

In the late 1970's a boss of mine relished in firing someone on Friday afternoon. I would go into his office after he had fired someone and found him glowing with a big smile from his left ear all the way to his right one. I wish I had taken a photo of him at the time of his glory, because the rest of the time he was basically just a nasty old grump. What made his mental circuitry so different from mine? I believe it has much less to do with some learned brain circuitry than it does with who we were before we were born. It's an established fact that we develop from both nature and nurture. However, like a famous boxer once coined, "He brought me to the heights of pisstivity." I believe this anger, as expressed by this boxer, reflects a contract we made with ourselves when we came here.

What I'm referring to is that there is strong evidence for reincarnation that's irrefutable by author and researcher Ian Stevenson, a

Canadian-born psychiatrist who worked for the University of Virginia School of Medicine for fifty years and as chair of their department of psychiatry from 1957 to 1967. This is also supported by many children in the United States who have provided verifiable evidence of a past life. It's my belief that some of us have more "pisstivity" genes, or pisstivity propensity, than others when we come out of the birth canal, and maybe even more of it from being pissed on in a past life.

My message in this book is not an attempt to prove reincarnation or life after death. I will assume that you already know about Dannion Brinkley, Anita Moorjani, Pam Reynolds and others whose near-death experiences are well worth looking into. My goal is to provide evidence and reasons for how certain negative behaviors in our lives are manifest via brain studies and some DNA evidence that forms who we are. One can also invert this to address positive behaviors as well, but the title of this work is *Why People Fight*, and not *Why People Love* (although this might be interesting research).

What is it that makes us individuals that believe in our own superiority and look down on the inferiority of others? The poem written by John Donne, *No Man Is an Island*, was written to convey that every person is a part of humanity. His thoughts reflect the universal connection with life being a single thread and that any man's death diminishes mankind. There is a flip side to every thought and concept. Although he is spiritually correct in that we are all connected, there is also a disconnect that we experience when disposed into this physical existence. Spiritually, we are one of the same fluidity of spiritual connectivity, even if we are not aware of it. The life force, if we can call it that, originates with a source and we are all connected to it and each other. In these physical containers, we have chosen to temporarily relinquish knowledge of our spiritual existence in order to experience a coarse existence within a thick and resistive environment—this physical plane.

This Universe has been created with the intent of supplanting within its bounds the essence of spiritual life, but with limitations in order to experience that which the nonphysical cannot deliver. In short, we can't physically fight there, in the spiritual plane, but we can here. There is no misunderstanding there, but there is here—maybe way too much of it, but couldn't that just be the plan?

The knowledge of our previous existence in the nonphysical that's been removed leaves us with only one aspect of that life force; that is, that we have the spirit of God inside ourselves but with some missing attributes and lots of missing knowledge. We are self aware with a force that is a remnant of God's omnipotence, yet depraved with a limited capacity to love and "walk a mile in another Indian's moccasins"—a line in a poem written by Mary T. Lathrap in 1895. This can be both a blessing and a hindrance. The good part is that we have been endowed with traits of compassion and love among many other emotions. The downside is that we can also believe that we are the center of correctness, that we cannot be wrong because we possess, in essence, a mini-god-like trait because God is our source and we therefore contain these critical remnants of being the masters of our own existence. That makes us perfect within our self-perception because God is perfect love, knowledge and power. But if we are perfect in respect that this is the plan and objective within our physical experience, why do we believe ourselves to be perfect, or that our inner beliefs at least are perfect? Why do we as a human species continue to fight? One clue is that we have within our genetics a fight-or-flight instinct with which we're all born and choose to exercise at will.

We Simply Can't Be Wrong

"Who decides whether something is right or wrong?" The best answer therefore must be, "We do."

We process a lot of data with that biochemical computer in our heads. It's said that it's capable of doing 100 trillion instruction processes per second with 100 trillion synapses equivalent to 100 million megabytes. Even with all this data processing ability, it's still not capable of making sense of everything that goes on around us. As we grow from childhood, we learn about our surroundings as if that's the way it is and nothing outside of what we have experienced has made its way into that perception of our world. Our personal Universe is fully encapsulated within that content. The longer we are alive, the larger that content grows. Some of us accept change and some of us only want to learn what supports what's already in there. This may or may not change our beliefs about God, Santa Claus, the Easter Bunny or the Boogeyman. It merely provides us with more data upon which to base our beliefs. Hence, we develop cognitive biases about many subjects that may or may not be true or correct. But within the structure of our belief system, these biases will stand up and fight against any data that may contradict them.

No matter how correct or incorrect these cognitive biases are, they will always present themselves as being right. These biases are our only means for making judgments over situations, from trivial ones to more serious to determine whether we fight or flee, agree or disagree and so on. They are the seat of our prejudices and the springboard for acceptance of any new truths, whether actually true or not. This mechanism is tainted with the belief that firstly we are inherently infallible at a rudimentary core that stems from our source. Therefore, what we tend to look for are confirmations to our biases, and mostly or completely dismissing anything that goes contrary to them. Hence, we reinforce our biases by attaching supporting data that agrees with us. The dumb may get dumber and the smart may get smarter, depending on your original biased points of view. This leads to a mindset that deepens its grooves, remains in the rut, and therefore we end up going to the same restaurants, wear the same type of clothing, maintain routines, engage in the same arguments and fight with the same foes.

A real danger to this is that one can fall into the trappings of quick decision-making based on past experiences that may lead us into hot water, dead ends and conflicts rather than seeing new and untried directions. The past does not always reflect the future. My nephew had made friends with some shady, tattooed ruffians that were initially outwardly friendly toward him. Based on this bias, he went to befriend a similar-looking group of guys who briskly threw him off a cliff and, thinking they had killed him, broke into his van to steal it. He survived, and has now changed that bias based on the color of his bruises and the cost of a new shirt and pants. Preconceived stereotypes provide a shortcut to decision making. This makes us jump to conclusions that may or may not serve us well. This heuristic is present when confronted with new experiences that guide us in making decisions.

Reaching conclusions without all the facts can get you thrown off a cliff, so to speak. If one applies good logic to false evidence, being right in a decision that's made may not serve one in a positive way. The same goes with fallacies in arguments over any subject. Anyone skilled in the art of rhetoric may also sway biases into a different direction that takes one's bias from true to false. This depends on the amount of weight that has been placed on past events and knowledge. If an event has occurred over and over, the odds of changing your bias concerning repeated past events would be low. Therefore, the frequency of something is proportional to how strong that bias will be. Another fact-avoidance tendency is when a majority of people has the same bias and you are outside their belief. In this case, there is a strong tendency to change and conform. There is a strong tendency to be a victim of your own false biases. The reality is that biases control behavior. Being right on an issue doesn't make one right since that issue itself may be false. Being right merely represents one's bias. It's one's belief on the issue that makes it right by the one believing, and not necessarily the issue.

No one believes they are wrong on any issue, and that's one of the challenges we face in dealing with people in our everyday lives. If one were to ask, "Who decides whether something is right or wrong?" The best answer therefore must be, "We do." This precludes the liar who is always wrong in that the lie itself is false, but that the motive may remain as a form of self-preservation or exaltation. In this case, the liar justifies being right.

There is no question about the rightness of morality. This is not the issue, but I will bring it up since many believe that it is not moral to kill, yet lives are taken every day in wars around the world and in senseless acts of violence over a moral issue. In war, the issue of morality is overshadowed by the purpose for which the person doing the killing is right in doing so. Fighting for freedom, over a religious ideology or fighting for your own life is a justifiably right act in the mind of the fighter. In many cases there is remorse in the afterthoughts when reflecting on their actions. This is when one right action is replaced with a right thought that can usher feelings of guilt, remorse or the feeling of wanting to make what is later viewed as wrong, right.

The extreme example of being right can be exemplified in the behavior of the psychopath. The psychopath always makes a deliberate choice for bad behavior and never a compulsive decision. When a psychopath is incarcerated for a crime, they sometimes will become indignant about it. They don't always realize that they have been caught for doing something bad and feel that the punishment is undeserved. Their thinking is that they have the correct rules and suddenly they are told that they are wrong and that there is another set of rules. In their thinking, this other set of rules is what's inappropriate. Their over-optimism makes them believe that their behavior, no matter how bad it may be, will always be rewarded and they don't pay much attention to punishment. Even the nonviolent psychopath that leads a normal life, holds a job and is an apparent upstanding member of the community will think very differently from neurotypicals. The upstanding psychopath sees them as unbearably and wastefully encumbered by guilt, shame, pity and fear. In other words, they always view their behavior as right, no matter how wrong it might be in the eyes of socially acceptable behavior.

To a lesser degree, we are all psychopathic. Psychopathy is not a condition with a clear line of demarcation between one diagnosed with the condition and a normal person. Psychopathy and sociopathy are sometimes used interchangeably, where the sociopath is considered to exhibit more antisocial behavior. Both are characterized by a disregard for the feelings of others. There's what is called the Hare Psychopathy Checklist, a psychological assessment tool used to assess the presence of psychopathy in individuals. The factors on this checklist do not determine a black-and-white characterization of the disorder, and therefore fall under much criticism. Some researchers suggest that the ratings often depend on the personality of the person doing the rating, which to some degree ignores etiology, the root cause. Some of the criteria that indicate a psychotic disorder could also be signs of mania, hypomania, frontal lobe dysfunction and even simple irresponsibility.

Being right about something connotes that we may also have a choice between right and wrong. This may not be the case at all with the psychopath, who does not make choices based on whether his or her choice is the right one. It's not well understood as to whether the psychopath has choices in their proclivities. Not knowing what it's like to "feel" may provoke insatiable desires toward violence and destruction, possibly as a sort of venting or simply believing it a good idea. What is difficult for them is to go out into society and mask themselves as being social. For them, feelings only get in the way of the moves they need to make. Being right is their normal; no matter what moves they make they will believe themselves to be "normal." Therefore, they too are never wrong.

This is referred to as egosyntonic, where it is prominently displayed that they see their antisocial behavior as justified. Their view of the neurotypicals is that they are weak, recognizing that their behavior is different. Therefore, the psychopath is difficult to treat, being only superficially cooperative and viewing the treatment as manipulative. It would be no surprise that the psychopath, knowing that they are different, would make the choice not to be cured—being right, and knowing it is a comfortable place to be.

If you don't believe me when I say that we are always right, as an exercise for yourself, try to make a wrong decision. I don't mean you should go out and rob a liquor store or pee on your boss's leg; we all know that these are wrong by legal and social standards. However, in your mind, try to make a wrong decision about your finances or doing something at work that will be wrong and cause you grief that you don't actually want. Deliberately attempting to make a wrong decision runs against our natural grain and should make one very uncomfortable. One may think of suicide as being a wrong decision; however, many view suicide as an act of "I win, you lose" by the person committing it. Checking out of a bad situation is viewed by them as the right decision, but without thinking through the ramifications to those left behind, and therefore it is a selfish decision.

All that can be said is that being right all the time doesn't necessarily belong to a disorder, but may be attributed to the claims of this writing, and that we are all subject to it. In summary, we are all subjects of our own rightness. The major difference between what can be categorized as normal and the psychopath is how quickly we can assess that we were wrong about something, and now have made a new right based on how well we can accept the new evidence to the contrary.

Since we are always right, but we also all have a different set of facts to support our rightness, what makes us fight over one person's right against another person's right?

The Psychology Of Lying

How ridiculous would it be for a mom, watching their child writhe in silence to such a question, say, "Oh, don't pay any attention, my kid's just learning how to lie."

Sociologists and psychiatrists support lying; well, at least to a certain degree. This may come as a shock to some people. Arnold Goldberg, a professor of psychiatry at Rush Medical College in Chicago, stated that, "Lying is as much a part of normal growth and development as telling the truth." He goes on to say, "The ability to lie is a human achievement, one of those abilities that tends to set them apart from all other species." Their studies focused on how and why children learn to lie. They viewed a child's first lie as a personal milestone in mental growth. Another study found that adults, on average, admitted to doing so thirteen times per week! Have we become a society of liars, or has it always been this way?

Today's psychiatrists only see lying as pathological when it becomes persistent. This is when it grows to a point that it's damaging not only in the liar's life but also those to whom they lie. A specific form of lying that a person will engage in is called pseudologia fantastica (why couldn't they just say "fantastic fake logic"?) and is usually easy to spot. This is when a person concocts a stream of tales in which a kernel of truth is intertwined for the purpose of self-aggrandizing. It's the old three-pound fish story that fantastically grew to ten pounds, with a pound or two being added with each reiteration. And what's more, it was caught during the worst storm of the century—in a leaking boat! I don't dare use the tale of a certain person exiting a helicopter under fire, ducking bullets. Pathological liars will appear as utterly sincere about their lies. These have believable consistency and for the tale-tellers, they don't seem to be able to monitor whether or not they are telling the truth themselves. These can be attributed to neurological difficulties.

Dr. Brian King, a psychiatrist at the David Geffen School of Medicine at UCLA, has categorized lies into five personality problems. These are manipulative, melodramatic, grandiose, evasive and guilty secrets. This research has concluded that lying plays a critical role in a child's development in that by the age of two, they experience that their parents are not all-knowing. They believe that this leads to the understanding that they are a separate person with a will of their own and can get away with things. They develop the perspective that they are in control of their emotions. They expound that by the ages between two and four, they have mastered the art of lying.

Since these studies were done in the United States and England, psychologists do not know how these apply to other cultures. I would say lying is pretty universal, but I would love to sign up for a government grant to study this on the island of Santorini for a year or two. If you've read my books before, you know how I feel about government-funded superfluous studies over issues that anybody with a modicum of common sense already knows.

Another study was conducted using three-year-olds. In this experiment, a toy was placed behind them and they were told not to look at the toy. The result was that only ten percent did not peek. Of the remainder, all turned around and looked at the toy. Of this group, about one-third admitted that they peeked at the toy; another third lied and said they did not peek, and the remaining third refused to say. Their conclusion was that the last third were learning to lie. I say, WTF? These guys touched a nerve with me on this conclusion!

Can children be baited in such a way as to support conclusions that place them headfirst into their innate insatiable curiosity? They are here in life to learn and experience. They have a built-in motivation to see, touch, smell, taste and hear every part of what this new existence has in store. To tell a child not to do something, and fully expect any other conclusion than some will and some won't, should be obvious. To add a vice grip to their innate desires that will force them to tell the truth, lie or simply put them on the spot to hear terrible silence just so you can collect a paycheck is, in my personal bias, deplorable. Any mother or father who's anywhere close to their child will come up with a different conclusion about the silent child. How ridiculous would it be for a mom, watching their child writhe in silence to such a question, say, "Oh, don't pay any attention, my kid's just learning how to lie."

I have to vehemently disagree with this conclusion; however, that's simply my opinion, and you know what they say about opinions. For all the people that didn't grow up in this country, opinions are like sphincters, everyone has one. Maybe *some* were "learning," or in the *process* of learning to lie, but from my own personal self-evaluation, I've actually been in a near exact situation as a four-year-old, and this is where psychologists and I part ways. Next to studying lying children on Santorini, I would love to receive a government grant to study psychologists!

In my humble opinion, children are not naïve little rug-rats lacking the towering experience and wisdom of parents, teachers and systematized psychologists. Grown-ups mostly forget their youth and what it was like being fresh and new, sharp as a tack with very astute powers of deduction. Adults tend to placate children or apply reasoning from their views over their behavior. Children may actually be more adept at life than adults that have collected lots of mental garbage over their timeline. There are some very interesting events that have happened in my childhood that puzzle me and have put me on the defense of children.

I have an excellent memory of my childhood. I can remember many situations when we lived in Canada, and I was only five years old when we moved from there to Ohio. I remember my grandmother's house with the clothesbasket at the end of an upstairs hallway. I can clearly see, in my mind's eye, the porch out front where they sat in rocking chairs. My grandmother's house burned down just before I was two years old!

When I was three years old, I was in a boat that turned over and everyone believed I had drowned. They looked for me for over thirty minutes, and finally decided to turn the boat right-side up in order to tie it back up to the dock. I had hung onto one of the seats while the boat was upside down; I can still see the greenish water I was in as I hung onto the seat with my little hands. After I was found, I clearly remember my grandmother and my aunt removing my wet clothes and drying me off after they had sat me on a kitchen counter. They asked me why I didn't answer to their calls, to which I responded, "I didn't want the fish would jump into my mouth." I remain in a state of amazement at children's astute powers of deduction!

What's also curious is the fact that I remember not being frightened, and more than anything else, I was extremely captivated by the beautiful color of the water. It's like I was just there, where I was supposed to be, and nowhere else. What I also remember very vividly was my grandfather, who was a very large, heavy man (fat, to be blunt), step off the pier and onto the beam. That's the very outer side of a small boat, if you aren't into boats. I somehow knew without a shadow of a doubt what was going to happen. With his heavy weight, the boat took a turn on its axis; Grandpa fell feet first into the water, Grandma went up in the air and kasplooshed into the water and I must have grabbed whatever I could hang on to. I don't remember exactly how I ended up hanging onto the seat, but I do remember most of what happened.

But, here's one for the books. I clearly remember riding in my stroller being pushed by my mom down the sidewalk. I recounted the appearance of that stroller many times. I recounted seeing the scenery, from my point of view, to my mom just a few years before she passed away. She looked at me with puzzled eyes and told me that this was not possible because I was no more than six months old. The more I described it, the more she became convinced that I did in fact remember many details of not only the stroller, but a large iron bar fence that we would pass during these strolls. I also told her about a large structure that looked like a government building not very far from our house. She confirmed that this was Societe Des Missions Etrangeres, a very large Catholic Society of Apostolic life for men that was just a few of blocks from where we lived. It was established in 1921 and does indeed look like a large government structure.

The stroller was blue and there were these fenders covering the wheels. At the very front was a tray where little toys could be carried, and right in the middle of this tray was a wooden T-bar handle I could put my hands on. The odd experience I had with this wooden handle still intrigues me. I remember wanting to turn right while being pushed on the sidewalk. Now, I don't remember why I wanted to turn right, I just remember clearly wanting to do so. I got a bit frustrated that the carriage did not respond to my physical pulling of my right hand and pushing of my left hand on this wooden handle bar, which should have made the carriage go right. I also got frustrated when the handle bar did not rotate like I thought it should. What's odd to me about this is, where did I ever get the notion that turning something in the direction I wanted to go might cause me to go in that direction? I've always thought this was strange, until I started my research into past life memories of children. Could this have been a carry-over from a past life in which I drove a car, and turning a wheel I had my hands on in front of me would allow me to turn where I wanted to go?

So, the idea of kids in general learning to lie just because some old farts with doctorate degrees say that's what is happening rubs me so wrong. I have vivid memories of what it was actually like being a toddler before I was two. It's my remembered experiences that differ greatly from the institutionally taught intelligentsia who probably don't remember anything before they were four—maybe even twenty-four.

Sigmund Freud coined the term "infantile amnesia." Very few people remember anything prior to three and a half years old. One researcher says that this is because there is little in the way of words that the child knows to associate an incident to. The Maori in New Zealand retain very early memories, going back to two and a half years old. It's believed that this is because the children are spoken to in a very elaborative manner. Experiences are shared with these children in richer, more detailed ways. I don't know why I have such early memories. In addition to that, my earliest memories don't relate to language, but more with curiosity about my surroundings. I didn't know enough to ask why grass was green; I just liked the color. I couldn't verbalize why I wanted to move around our house; all I remember is that I just wanted to.

In my mid-twenties, during a flat-track motorcycle race, I got a severe concussion from hitting my head on the hard track when I went down. I suffered total amnesia for several hours and partial amnesia for over a week. It took me three weeks before I could remember who I was calling in the time it took me to push the buttons on a phone. This feeling of being in an environment with no prior existence reminded me of when I was a very small child. The exception was that during my amnesia, I knew something was wrong. As a small child, there was no fear of anything until I became aware that there could be punishable consequences for certain actions. This seemed to have started late in my first year. By the time I was two and a half to three, I remember my dad disciplining me. I don't remember my mom disciplining me until I was about four.

When I was four years old, we lived at the shoe repair shop my father ran in Canada. I picked up my mom's expensive bottle of perfume and began to take a sip thinking that if it smells that good, it must also taste good. Of course, that was not the case. When my mom saw that some of it was missing, she asked me if I had spilled it playing in her bedroom. I refused to answer. Why did I refuse? One reason that I refused was because I didn't want to tell her that it was me that caused her to lose something precious to her. Mom was that special person in my limited universe. But mostly I refused to answer her because *I did not want to lie to my mom.* At four years old, I instinctively knew that lying was wrong. And what I know now is that I didn't care about learning to lie—period! In fact, I have the distinct gut feeling that I knew lying was wrong long before this. This is not to say that I did not lie as a child; I must have, although I don't recall any incident of lying. I would rather just keep my mouth shut if I thought I was in some sort of trouble. Lying always brought about a feeling of discomfort and I avoided it. I've lied much more in my adulthood, but since I was thirty-five, I vowed to always tell the truth no matter how much it bothered me. That's really, really hard to do!

I have many vivid memories of my childhood before I was five years old. I can say with conviction that there are some human traits that we don't *need* to learn, and I don't believe we, as a general premise, "learn" to lie or that lying plays a critical role in a child's development. I believe that we instinctively know the right and wrong of lying as our vocabulary increases. I also believe we come into this world with a large package of knowing. Lying, not lying or remaining silent when put on the spot, at least for me, was part of that package that was ingrained in me and also inside all those different little personalities that came here, just like me. We may also be instilled within certain personality types. It may be part of that same package to believe that just because you possess some sort of credential, that this will make one an authority that's going to be right.

When I say we instinctively know right from wrong, I'm not referring to kids just being curious about the world around them, or exhibiting what might be construed as bratty action by going around someone's house grabbing every knick-knack or expensive vase. Learning about our physical surroundings through our senses is separate from the innate deep-seated knowledge and emotions ingrained within our complex nature. Passion, love, anger, excitement, agitation and so on are exhibited very early. The mere act of going from quietude to crying at the time of birth is not a learned behavior. Babies will kick their little legs in joy and, as my kids did very early on, gaze at their little fingers in what looks like total amazement. It was like they just knew they were here. In my mind, I thought, what else do they know? I don't think babies are born with nothing in there. Even baby sea turtles know what direction to go in after they break out of their egg shells, and what's more, like babies, they instinctively know how to swim—although many forget by the time they're able to walk and run.

It's my opinion that research into child behavior comes from a tainted perspective—not always, but too often. One researcher, whose name I won't mention, is quoted as saying of children two to four years old, "Children at that age are fine-tuning their superego, or consciousness." He further says, "The first evidence of pathological lying shows up during these years, in children who have a faulty superego and think they can get away with anything." A faulty superego? Maybe . . . but that statement really pisses me off! Another researcher said, "If a child did not develop the abilities that allow him to lie, he would remain immature." He's full of crap! This is really cause for me to contact this idiot and tell him to get a life!

What goes on inside the mind of another is too often skewed, or more so, screwed up by the mind of the one analyzing the other. I'm sure to receive some shit from all these cretins accusing me of not having a degree in child psychology, but I'm so qualified from the standpoint that I once was a child, and remember it very well! It's also my opinion that too many of these self-appointed hypocrite grown-ups are so disconnected with their childhood that they don't know jack shit, believing that children are naïve and that only grown-ups know everything about everything. I must point out that children are a hell of a lot smarter than we give them credit for. They recently came from a place we have forgotten and arrive with a full set of tools that we, as grown-ups, totally fail to recognize and have totally disconnected from. That does not forego discipline and guidance, but it does suggest that we grown-ups would fare well to get in tune with our kids by engaging ourselves in some of their stranger activities, and to hell with this grown-up crap. As they get into their teens, the generation gap widens and all we grown-ups can do is bitch, bitch, bitch at them. They don't want to have Mom or Dad badgering them day and night for any reason. I won't go into the psychology of raising teenagers, but I know that this is a time when kids and parents part ways. It's like the sign I once read in the lobby of one of my clients that read, "Hire a teenager while they still know everything." I could punch some of these assholes right in the face if I ever got close to one of them!

Well… I'm sure you noticed a change in tone in my explosive expletives and verbalization about child psychologists, right? I bet you thought I had gone a bit off my rocker, didn't you? This is an example of adhering to a belief to the point of escalating anger that then leads to explosive anger, infuriation, rage and finally aggression. It's a trap we've all fallen into at some time or other. It's called the anger escalation process. It may take minutes, hours, days or even months. In my case above, it took only a few paragraphs to illustrate anger escalation. I bet if you are a psychologist, or worse, a child psychologist reading my bit, you were getting ready to give me a call or catch me in the parking lot with a baseball bat. To anyone I might have offended, I sincerely apologize. But still I must ask, is lying healthy?

In my random internet research on lying, I humorously found these two views. Under the heading "Lying Is Good For You," they state, "And lying has proven psychological benefits. For instance, there's scientific evidence showing that depressive people are more honest with themselves than nondepressive, or mentally healthy, people." Right under that Google search heading was, "We established very clearly that purposefully trying not to lie caused people to tell fewer lies. When they told more lies, their health went down. And when they told the truth, it improved." I actually get a bit ruffled (no, I'm not going to go on a tirade again) when I hear that lying is good, and breathe a sigh of relief when I read about a researcher that agrees with my beliefs—that lying is not so good. Right under these two headings were these: "Lying is Absolutely Necessary," "Want a Healthier Longer Life? Stop Lying," "When Lying is Good," and "The Truth Is, Lying Makes You Sick." Oh gosh, what to do, what to do?

It's quite easy to point to someone else's behavior and draw conclusions, and that's notwithstanding any particular group. The fact is that we never know what's inside another's thoughts. Outward behavior often does not reflect who the actual person is inside their thinking self. For example, I had a friend with unusually long hair when long hair was considered unacceptable. This was in Mississippi, and it was really frowned upon in that particular part of the country. It was in the early sixties and if you had long hair, you were considered dirty, deplorable and someone to avoid. Another friend of mine who was a police officer that I rode dirt bikes with came to our house when my long-haired "hippie" friend happened to be there. When these two met, the officer glared at him and began to psychoanalyze the reason for the long hair.

He began with his belief that the long hair represented a form of rebellion. He went on to explain that this was to exhibit individuality as a person that's set apart from the rest of society. The hair, for him, also represented a disapproval of the status quo; that it was a display of a movement that was to take a new place in society. It was also a display of his freedom to choose for himself the kind of life he wanted that was unique, as in some art form, and on and on.

My friend listened for quite some time, letting the policeman exhaust his analysis. He then said, "No, it's none of those reasons. It's because I like it." I believe he was telling the absolute truth, but my police officer friend wasn't buying it.

Analyzing why children and people in general lie will always be tainted with the colored glasses through which the analyst is peering. In a similar way that the psychopath is analyzed using the Hare Psychopathy Checklist, with its critics wearing a different set of glasses, so too the reasons for lying can be merely one's opinion from an outside perspective. The finality is that people lie, and sometimes it really pisses others off when they are lied to.

No matter how it's sliced and diced, being lied to is a self-justified reason for anger and conflict, and one of the reasons why we might choose to fight.

Our Reaction To Annoyances Could Be Genetic

Annoyance makes me think of the Steve Allen, Steve Lawrence, Eydie Gormé and Ann Sothern song, "This Could Be the Start of Something Big."

Being annoyed is being slightly angry. It could be a prelude to outright anger and an escalation to fighting if left turned on for long enough. The threshold between being annoyed and angry enough to take some undesirable action varies greatly from person to person. Some people will trip at a glance, while others will take the annoying abuse for long periods before finally commenting on it or actually blowing up.

But what if someone is annoyed with you? Even very nice people can annoy others without ever knowing it. I once heard someone say, "She really makes me mad. She's so perfect, so nice. I can't stand her." What if you were a mind reader able to detect when you are annoying someone else even if you're "so perfect, so nice"? Since most of us can't read minds, might it be better if a person told you that you were annoying them before the situation got out of hand? What should one look for when interacting with someone or even minding their own business that would stave off a potential conflict sparked by a little annoyance?

If you're engaged with someone and they become silent or unresponsive, you may become annoyed with their lack of engagement. You may not realize you are the source of annoyance and getting on their nerves. I would watch for crossed arms, wincing, huffing, sighing, their eyebrows pinched together, or looking in a different direction than straight on. It's my advice, if you notice any of the annoyed-type body language, to avoid asking another person if you're annoying them. This might be a recipe for retaliation. Put another way, NEVER say, "Am I fucking annoying you?" Jeez, this is my third book and the first time I've used the "F" word. I hope this hasn't annoyed you.

Annoying people are inevitable, and annoying people is inevitable. Some people are just born with optical rectitis. This is when the optic nerve gets crossed with the nerves of the rectum and one develops a shitty outlook on life. Either these people are going to annoy you or you are going to annoy them. Our birth programming and nature's molding inhibits our ability to be compatible with everyone. In fact, we are so individualized that it's virtually an impossibility to find anyone that doesn't annoy us at some point or another. The most compatible of marriages will have some quirk that leads to a disagreement, even though they may be small and far between. Most couples find that their first year is the worst. That's when they discover the other's unknown quirks. What's interesting about being with someone is that the longer we are together, one of two things occurs. We will come closer with fewer disagreements or we will increase our differences, leading to fights, verbally and sometimes, unfortunately, physically. Few relationships remain the same over long periods of time—some improve while others go down the tubes and some, like older couples that are even cute in their *forever bickering*, remain in a constant state—can't live with 'em, can't live without 'em.

When couples have their fights, it often revolves around the same issues. This could be the darker side of love, and sometimes fighting is actually what keeps couples together. It's like the sadist that once said, "You can't hurt me; I like pain." Some people just aren't happy unless they're miserable. Yes, that's actually a true statement. You can buy a t-shirt online with that on it. The thing that amazes me about couples fighting that I found in my research is that 69% of marriage conflicts are never resolved. This is probably why they revolve around the same issues. We never have enough money. That's because we spend more than we make. Since we spend more than we make, we never have enough money. What most often happens is that there is something that annoys us; therefore, we focus on it. Focusing on it brings it to the forefront. The more it's brought to the forefront, the bigger the issue becomes until one or the other snaps or decides it's time to take some action that will either resolve the issue, delete the issue or run away from it.

One definition of annoy is "to rouse to impatience or anger." Another is "to irritate or make someone a little angry." These definitions fail to further define the emotion as part of the spectrum from calm to violent. Annoyance makes me think of the Steve Allen, Steve Lawrence, Eydie Gormé and Ann Sothern song, "This Could Be the Start of Something Big."

In 1931, Adolf Hitler was very annoyed when a Jewish lawyer named Hans Litten confronted him in court. During the trial against four members of the Nazi Party's Sturmabteilung paramilitary group, in which three people were killed, Hitler was summoned as a witness. Hitler was interrogated in a calm and methodical manner that was contrary to his confrontational approach to arguments. Litten's precise and detailed questioning dismantled all claims by Hitler that he was committed to "100% legality." The crack in the dike began to widen when Litten asked why armed men had accompanied him. Hitler raised his voice, shouting back, "That's complete lunacy!"

But Litten didn't stop. He asked Hitler why Goebbels made assertions that the Nazi movement would "make revolution" and "chase parliament to the devil" using "German fists." This made Hitler stammer and, according to a contemporary newspaper, he began to "search convulsively for an answer." According to some historians, it was not so much that Litten was a Jew, but that there was someone that was talking calmly and coolly to him that drove Hitler berserk.

Hitler basically blamed Jewish bankers for losing World War I, but being annoyed with Hans Litten must have surely left an indelible mark on his stewing memory. Litten was sent to three different concentration camps, where he was repeatedly beaten and, when he couldn't endure it any longer, he took his own life by hanging himself in 1938.

There's an online naval action game that's popular. In one of their forums there's a post where players can vet out their major annoyances. Here are a few: "being dragged in a battle without the opportunity to decline"; "Shallows that make it difficult to enter in a deep port"; "No telescope on the open sea, I'd like to zoom in on islands." What if these people could be transported back in time and had these same annoyances during a real battle between the USS Constitution and HMS Guerriere? What would have actually happened if Captain James Richard Dacres of HMS Guerriere might have said to Captain Isaac Hull of the Constitution, "Oh, well, I choose to decline engaging in this battle"? Or, during the battle of Köge Bay when two large ships ran aground, what if those captains had requested that they hold off the battle until the dredges arrived to scoop out the bottom? Or better yet, what could be more annoying than being an ancient Egyptian captain really annoyed because he didn't have a telescope to view islands in the Mediterranean? It even annoys me to learn of people's annoyances today when things should be so much better than it was when life was much more difficult and, I might add, annoying. What does that tell us? Have we come a long way in technology only to become incapacitated of our innate human paradigm of intolerance to simple annoyances?

In the International Journal of Conflict Management it was learned that one was more likely to blame the person causing the annoyance over the fact that the person being annoyed also escalated the annoyance into a conflict. They also learned, from a study of what causes annoyances, that even neutral stimuli or one that may be pleasant can become annoying when encountered over and over again. It's like listening to that annoying guy on the TV or radio that plays his commercial so many times that you just want to strangle him! There's one here in Los Angeles where this guy says over and over again, "You're killing me Harry." I just wish he'd actually do it! (Just kidding, of course. Please don't sue.)

There are several medical causes for irritability that trigger annoyances. An overactive thyroid, called hyperthyroidism, which is more common in women, can be a reason for consistently being agitated. It affects metabolism and can cause nervousness and affect concentration.

Depression can lead to aggression, anger and can trigger panic attacks. A study conducted by the University of California found that statins, which are widely prescribed to treat high cholesterol, lower serotonin, which can increase anger and depression. And lastly, Mother Nature occasionally upsets the hormones estrogen and progesterone, making women more irritable, hence increasing anger. Many conditions affect the serotonin level in the brain, which has a direct effect on one's happy scale.

Some people are born with such a low tolerance for anything that annoys them that they are prone to leading a life of crime. In the late 1800's, the Italian criminologist and physician Cesare Lombroso popularized the idea that criminal behavior is inherited. His theory was mostly discarded due to lack of evidence, but it was revived in the 1970's when it was discovered that men with an extra Y chromosome were especially violent. Although this discovery failed to provide support, a later study provided evidence that those with the XYY chromosome were more likely to have an arrest record than those that did not. What this suggests was that the evidence is consistent that genetics is a factor in the assessment of what causes crime.

A study led by the Karolinska Institute in Sweden found that 10% of all violent offenders had the MAOA and CDH13 genes, while nonviolent offenders did not. Although this study is significant, the majority of people who carry both these genes do not commit violent crimes. This doesn't mean that these are the "crime genes," but makes it worthwhile to look for biological contributions to antisocial behavior.

In a more recent study, it was found that the MAOA gene, monoamine oxidase A, has two variants—L and H. This growing study suggests that MAOA-L produces a vulnerability toward violent behavior. They have termed it the "warrior gene." This does not suggest that if one has this gene that they will become violent; there are more complex genetic and environmental factors that affect behavior. There's more on this in a later chapter. It does suggest, however, that having this gene, you are more likely to head toward aggression, especially if you were mistreated as a child.

These findings, along with others that tie genetics with race, are a lightning rod for social activists. There are legal issues as to whether one is responsible for their crimes because they may have certain genetic propensities toward violence. Two academic books on the subject of violence were published with a violent backlash, and the Canadian government even banned one. Criminologist Dr. Ray Jeffery commented on the volatility of such research and stated that, "When it comes to unraveling the true nature of aggression, perhaps it's in our genes to do little more than fight about it."

Disputes Over Change

The adage, "If it ain't broke, don't fix it" can be an insurmountable resistance to change. In addition, predicting the far-reaching consequences of change can be nothing more than a crapshoot.

What makes one person love spaghetti will produce a grimace on the face of another. And, if you ask any Italian why that is, they will be perplexed that anyone would be repelled at the sight of a steaming tomato sauce and tender meatball plate of their signature delicacy. While sex is viewed as one of the most beautiful of experiences, some view it as dirty, repulsive. As likes and dislikes diverge, some people develop a propensity for aggression toward anyone that is not in lockstep with their approaches to life and preferences. Discord much too often produces more of the same. None could be more apparent than with religious and political stances. The thrust that others should run their lives in the same manner that we do can leave a mark of disdain on the disagreeable person. The real question should not be, "Why don't they see it my way?" but rather, "Why we have come to an impasse on any belief we who are on either side of an issue have inflated with supporting evidence that we are right and they are wrong?" What's more, in many cases, the opposing belief may have stemmed from someone that once believed as you do having now changed their position. What was once "us" has now become "them."

The year 2016 was a tumultuous but very interesting election year. As Hillary and Donald squared off in their last debate, they garnered 71.6 million viewers—according to one website. Here we go again with statistics. CNN's website says that this was the most-watched debate in history with well over 80 million. Nielsen's count was 84 million. Another says that the most watched debate was 80.6 million between Jimmy Carter and Ronald Reagan in 1980. The most watched broadcast in history is the Super Bowl XLIX (49) in 2014.

But, statistics aside … a whole lot of kids from my generation watched *The Howdy Doody Show* on Saturday morning, with Buffalo Bob Smith, Clarabell and the Flub-a-Dub. I was actually more entertained by *The Howdy Doody Show* than I was with the debates, which left me with the feeling that nothing that was said changed any decision that was made prior. For most people I've talked with, it was more rooting for your candidate, like watching Super Bowl XLIX. When Hillary scored, the Trumpers got quiet and the Hillary fans cheered. When Trump scored the opposite happened. So few beliefs were changed and therefore, the debates might as well never have taken place. In my opinion, it was more for the entertainment value and the money that was made by advertisers and the networks.

As it became evident that the big guy with the funny hair was winning and everyone in the girls' event hall were told to just go home, there was jubilation for the winner. There was also total dejection for the people that believed they were going to have a really big party that night. This was followed by disbelief later with the reality of a news scene of violence in which a man was videotaped being beaten on the street for voting for the winner. One group was very happy and the other was very angry—even angrier because the general consensus was that the losers were going to win big time. On that day, everything changed.

This exemplified a serious case of "us" and "them" over a perceived change from expectations. Today, while I'm in my office writing, the two teams are still squaring off, still hoping that she gets locked up and that he gets his "president" title revoked by impeachment or worse. Some of us get so wrapped up with life's events that it begins to control us. The fact is that most thoughts that intrude our consciousness are outside of our control due to some initial idea that has grown to gargantuan proportion over time. There's an old Chinese proverb that states, "Be careful of your thoughts, for your thoughts become your words. Be careful of your words, for your words become your actions. Be careful of your actions, for your actions become your habits. Be careful of your habits, for your habits become your character. Be careful of your character, for your character becomes your destiny." The original author is unknown, but these words are as relevant today as they were centuries ago.

Since the subconscious mind is like a computer taking for granted what it takes in as if it were a mere data-collection program, input about any subject will be cast literally as-is into the subconscious as fact without us being aware it's happening. This data is simply accepted and stored. Also, since the conscious mind is the gateway that makes a determination about the data stored in the subconscious as to whether to accept, reject or remain indifferent to it, we might think that we are in control of what we think. Of course, that's what makes us all "right" about everything. However, repetition can reinforce anything that is either wrong or doesn't make any sense. This is where we believe our thoughts belong to us whereas our thoughts, that which we believe, actually came from somewhere outside of us. In other words, we aren't who we think we are.

It's a human attribute, maybe even a peculiarity of our thought process, that we will initially oppose anything we encounter that doesn't agree with our belief system. The idea of change alone does not conflict with our beliefs. Beliefs welcome certain changes and are threatened by others that are in disagreement. However, change with a possible potential for benefit that neither agrees nor disagrees with beliefs will find a level of positive acceptance.

An experiment was conducted in the 1970's to find out what increased productivity in factories. Many factors of the factory environment were revised and productivity did in fact improve, but within a few months, it returned to its previous level. It was when they tried playing soothing background music that they made a profound discovery. When they began playing the music, productivity went up. After a period of time, productivity returned to the previous level, so they decided to turn it off. When they did this, productivity went up! The researchers then conducted several other experiments in which productivity went up upon instilling it, and then down after some time, whereupon removing the control of the experiment productivity would then again go back up.

Their conclusion was the fact that management was acting on the behalf of the employees by changing certain conditions, and the employees responded in kind. The deduction was that it was management's decision to make "changes" on behalf of the employees that increased productivity, not the change itself. However, changes that favored management reduced productivity.

Changes are resisted when we feel there's a loss of control and uncertainty. There's also a resistance when a change is a departure from the way it's been done, giving people the perception that they've been wrong all along. Sometimes the threat of change becomes real when negative results are realized. Resistance to change is often overarched by the unknown consequences of the change. The adage, "If it ain't broke, don't fix it" can be an insurmountable resistance to change. In addition, predicting the far-reaching consequences of change can be nothing more than a crapshoot.

One fundamental human need that can lead to conflict is identity. This is our sense of self. Any sense of threat to identity as a result of something changing is met with an aggressive form of defense. Identity is ingrained into our views of how things should be. It's our sense of control over our own lives. We all identify with those within our own group types. Identity is primarily responsible for ethnic and racial conflicts. Conversely, as a group we tend to view those with opposing views as oppressive social structures where identification becomes more polarized. High levels of identification can lead to perceived threats and a propensity to want to destroy the perceived opponent. Identity conflicts typically involve perceived injustice. If we even think a change is not in our interest, whether it is or not, it will be fought against. Perception is everything.

Belief systems become rigid when opposing views threaten to

change one or the other. Conflicts can arise over just about any issue, from religion to material things to insults. Should these opposing sides become unable to mitigate their differences, they begin to view each other as enemies. The issue then becomes irrelevant. It's the action taken against this enemy that intractably falls within a different order of human quirks, and that is whether the action results in victory or defeat. However, it doesn't always end so decisively. Should the victor take their action to extreme or inhumane treatment of their already defeated opponent, the antagonism deepens when the loser or his associates, relatives, etc. takes revenge. This escalation can grow into what the combatant factions feel is critical to their survival.

The basic instinct for survival is instilled in all living things and is a fundamental need. Imposing change on another's beliefs that escalates to physical conflict critical to their survival becomes intractable. Fear and hatred become ingrained with a total unwillingness to reconcile any differences. That's when change is most needed, but is most unlikely.

Why Tempers Flare

"That doesn't look like a real gorilla!" That's when your best friend's amygdala and prefrontal cortex work in concert to avert his own self-imposed threat. He throws up his hands to block your punch, but you pull back just in time. "Fred, what the hell are you doing in there?"

Many returning soldiers are very familiar with IEDs. These are improvised explosive devices that the enemy makes in their kitchen arsenal or living rooms using any unconventional military method. It may be constructed from a military explosive, such as an artillery round attached to a detonating mechanism, or components packed into a device that explodes out anything from nails to ball bearings. It can even be a radioactive dirty bomb. In the field of psychiatry, IED stands for "intermittent explosive disorder." Someone suffering from IED will exhibit behavior from wall-punching, object-throwing and tire-screeching to people-punching, people-throwing and people-stabbing—though it's called something more serious when there's people-stabbing.

What psychiatrists have discovered is that anger runs in families, pointing conclusively that genetics plays a role in IED. They have also discovered a relation between anger and the amygdala and the prefrontal cortex of the brain. The prefrontal cortex allows us to exercise control over our primitive angry impulses. This is where a threat is determined and an appropriate response to the threat is made.

Professor Adrian Raine, a psychologist at the University of Southern California, conducted a study of forty-one impulsive murderers, people who have killed in a fit of rage, to find out if their brains were physically different from normal people. What he wanted to learn is if their brains functioned differently when subjected to stress. What he discovered was that normal people exhibited high glucose metabolism or high brain functioning in the prefrontal cortex. In the brains of impulsive murderers, there was a distinct lack of activation in the prefrontal cortex, the part of the brain that controls and regulates behavior. What this says is that the individual that lacks normal brain activity in that region of the brain is more likely to lash out in a violent manner when agitated. These findings are provocative and controversial.

The amygdala is extremely efficient. In fact it warns us about threats before the prefrontal cortex can check on the reasonability of our reaction to it. It enables us to get pissed off before we have a chance to determine what level of "pisstivity" will be commensurate with the threat. Aside from the impulsive murderer, what more-or-less-normal people may actually do is react until there is some feedback from the frontal cortex. This can result in someone punching a perceived threat in the face (actually saw this on a YouTube video) not fully realizing that it was his best friend dressed in a gorilla suit playing a joke on him.

During this time, inside the brain, neurotransmitter chemicals known as catecholamines are released, leaving you with a burst of energy so you can protect yourself against fake gorillas. Since you don't know it's fake, your heart accelerates, blood pressure rises and breathing rate increases. Your face gets red, your attention narrows, you lock onto the gorilla's face and everything else seems to disappear. Your adrenaline and noradrenaline turn you into a fighting machine ready to take on the hairiest of opponents. The amygdala has heightened your emotion. Now it's time to think, and that's when your left prefrontal cortex switches off the heightened emotion. "That doesn't look like a real gorilla!" That's when your best friend's amygdala and prefrontal cortex work in concert to avert his own self-imposed threat. He throws up his hands to block your punch, but you pull back just in time. "Fred, what the hell are you doing in there?"

For the impulsive murderer, the story does not have a happy ending. The prefrontal cortex is slow to decide, if it does at all, and the state of anger persists. The gorilla remains an object of anger and is killed with his best friend inside—oops. The lingering anger can also interfere with memory, and details of the outburst remain blurred. Certain levels of arousal can benefit memory but high levels, such as those present in a state of anger, can impair one's ability to concentrate. We become reactionary, and memory of an explosive event is difficult.

A contributor to anger is low levels of serotonin. According to research performed at Cambridge's Behavioral and Clinical Neuroscience Institute of Zurich, it's been known for decades that serotonin plays a key role in aggressive behavior, but it's only recently that the technology has enabled researchers to understand how. In one aggressive behavioral study, volunteers had their diets altered with a mixture of amino acids that lacked tryptophan, the building block for serotonin. What they found during brain scans of the subjects was that low brain serotonin made communication between the amygdala and the frontal lobes weaker compared to normal levels of serotonin. This made it more difficult for the prefrontal cortex to control emotional responses to anger generated by the amygdala.

Another study on aggressive behavior was the tDCS (transcranial direct-current stimulation) with which they have concluded that individuals who received tDCS to increase relative left frontal cortical activity behaved more aggressively when they were angry. No relation between anger and aggression was observed in the increased relative right frontal cortical activity condition.

Although research in brain activity has located regions and connections within these that are biologically connected with anger and even explosive anger, other researchers have found psychological connections associated with anger.

Narcissism and inflated ego syndrome characterize a person that can't be wrong about anything. Others have no right to question or object to anything they say. These people will defend their stance right to the end because they can never admit to making any mistakes. They will egotistically admire their own attributes. It's actually a social problem in relationships with others and even with oneself. If the narcissist detects a perceived threat he may turn to narcissistic rage, which can range from mild irritation to violent attacks. Narcissism comes in many varieties that are referred to as narcissistic inventory. These include:

1. Defending one's self worth is an action where one will not care so much about the topic as much as they wish to prove that they aren't ignorant of the topic.

2. Defending a belief is an action where one will become anything but rational while defending a belief that is of a personal matter. This is when an intelligent adult will be no more intelligent than their elementary school child when defending this sort of belief that matters to their well being.

3. Craving superiority is an action where one will search for any way to disagree just to feel superior. By proving others wrong, they will feel superior. If challenge is persistent, anger will erupt.

Some people just have hatred for anyone disagreeing with them. In contrast to love, history has given a miniscule amount of attention to hate. In a survey of social psychology texts, love has an index term in every one reviewed, while hate had none. One definition of hate I recently read was that, "hate is a self-destructive emotion turned outward."

A rather convoluted definition of hate from The Chicago School of Professional Psychology says, "Hate by itself is the emotional dynamic of the ability to sustain long periods of concentration and meditation. It does not require an object to focus on (it mirrors pure love in this respect); it is a general-purpose tool for cutting positive attachments, especially in relationships (for example, pride in hate mode rejects another person, whereas hate by itself rejects any pleasant attachment to the other person). Hate produces clear thinking and strengthens a person's will power. It supports the desire for solitude. It cools the mind and may easily be mistaken for a mild sense of peace. It is likely to be the prevailing mood when a mediator claims that they are no longer acting from a sense of ego. The skilful way of using hate is to clear the mind of redundant attachments and desires."

Holy moly! There's a lot to be said about that one! "Hate produces clear thinking"??? "It cools the mind and may easily be mistaken for a mild sense of peace"??? "It's a general-purpose tool for cutting positive attachments…"??? "It does not require an object to focus on"??? After I read this, I told my wife to never go to a psychologist—for anything!

It's perfectly okay to disagree with me on what I'm about to say, and I'll probably get some hate mail from The Chicago School of Professional Psychology, but…Firstly, the clear thinking bit: when I'm working on something important and my computer locks up, and I lose data, I really hate that! In fact, I get so fuzzy in the brain that I actually have contemplated getting a hammer and literally destroying that little box. What's even worse is I can imagine Bill Gates being inside it when I smash its electronic brain in. Then, after the hate subsides, I get a little clearer and think, "That's a tool I paid good money for. What the hell was I thinking? And Bill Gates may not be all *that* bad."

About cooling the mind and mistaking hate for a mild sense of peace, well, for me, that's totally out of the question. If I hate it when a client starts yelling at me for something I didn't do, I have absolutely no sense of peace. My mind is anything but cool. In fact, I can get pretty hot when I hate it when shit happens. After all, I'm just as human as you and them, whoever they are.

As for it being a general-purpose tool for cutting positive attachments, well, this makes no sense at all. Why in blazes would you want to cut these "positive attachments," especially with hate? Why would anyone introduce hate into anything positive?

If it doesn't require an object to focus on, that would mean that one can just hate a great big general nothing—just sit there hating with absolutely nothing to hate. This absolutely makes no sense.

In researching hate, I've learned that there are many ambiguous and conflicting takes on it. Things like "haters are all insecure." "Haters like to hate in groups." Then there are in-groups and out-groups that always hate each other. There's the guy that said that "people confuse jealousy and envy with hate." And, "Hate is not the opposite of love." Most of which is opinion. And I found this astute statement from a director of a famous institute that I won't mention: "Hate is a brain function, so you can't see it in the brain when the brain is not functioning due to death." Hmmm … due to death? Gosh, I never would have thought of that.

More logical reasons for hate more likely stem from more logical people with more logical perceptions. Professors Semir Zeki and John Romaya did another study of hate and haters that, to me, has more substance, performed at Wellcome Laboratory of Neurobiology at University College London. Their claim is that they may have found a hate circuit in the brain. Their study involved seventeen subjects that had their brains scanned while looking at photos of people they grossly disliked. What they found was that this hate circuit is distinct from those that relate to danger, threat or fear. It also shares two common structures with the romantic love circuit, but it is quite distinct. This hate circuit involves two parts of the brain known as the putamen and the insula. These are also the parts of the brain associated with love, but in the case of love, different areas of the prefrontal cortex become deactivated. Tempers flare when this hate circuit generates a behavior of aggression, and bad things happen when it translates it into action.

The conclusions we can draw from these studies of the brain is that certain areas of the brain activate according to certain emotions. Love and hate are close cousins with subtle but distinct differences. What is not asked is comparable to the old question of what came first, the chicken or the egg? Is it the brain's collective data that triggers it to become active in certain hate-centered areas, or is it an invisible, intangible us, the id—that seat of emotion that changes the condition of certain circuits of the brain? If we are merely brain data since birth, it's no wonder that we would disagree with what another's data comprises. We can't know everything. In fact, most of us know nearly nothing when compared to the collective available knowledge that's been documented in the annals of human history. I would even go so far as to say that much of this knowledge isn't even accurate. How many times have we heard from a History Channel TV show that this new information could rewrite history?

Whether it's different and opposing stored data between individuals or groups, chemical changes in our biological system, brain wiring we can't control or some preprogrammed id we came into this world with, anger erupts under a very wide variety of circumstances. The question of this work is not that we disagree and get angry, but why do so many of us resort to fighting, either verbally or physically, rather than accepting our differences? That's a line I've heard over and over again, this "accepting our differences" bit that appears to be much more ignored by society than accepted. We staunchly make footholds in our beliefs and our approaches to the way things should be, reinforce them with data that agrees with these beliefs, dwell on them to make them even bigger than life and when any action violates them, our "pisstivity" circuit lights up and tempers flare.

Animals Fight Too

Therefore, you might say that there's one characteristic bonobos share with humans—they have sex for pleasure and possibly entertainment as well as to propagate the species.

We diverge in our preferences, ideologies, likes and dislikes from the time we begin to make sense of the environment we've been exposed to. Birth begins the journey of life and experiences. Death, in my belief system, allows us to bring the experiences of a lifetime, no matter how long or short, into a vast storage of collective human and animal experiences. Animals are no different from us in their experience of life. This is supported by many reports of ghostly apparitions of deceased pets and people briefly reunited with pets in near-death experiences.

Let's start with cats. Cats will vehemently defend their turf. They are very territorial and will not be very receptive to another cat, especially if they are both males. Even two cats in the same household offer no guarantee that they will get along. Unneutered cats will threaten another male over a female. Should they engage in an actual fight, they can make quite a racket with their howling and screaming that can wake up the entire neighborhood. Cat behaviorists claim that cats will vent aggression by redirecting it. For example, a housecat may see another cat or dog through a window. He begins to feel like his territory is being invaded, but can't get to the intruder. He then attacks another animal living in the house. Cats normally don't back down from a confrontation but would rather fight.

On the other hand, dogs are social animals much more willing to live in groups. Their ancestry allowed them to work together to kill food and also to defend their territory. Dog aggression can occur when a dog is not well socialized and will have more difficulty interpreting another's intent. Dogs are more prone to let things go when another dog reacts in a submissive posture. In packs, there emerges an alpha, or dominant dog in a clear hierarchy. Often fighting is the method for establishing this pecking order.

I was raised around animals and have experienced firsthand that all animals can be annoyed for one reason or another. I've also seen animals go from an annoyed state to an all-out fight. So, in this area, they aren't any different from us. On the flip side, I've experienced the loyalty of dogs I've had that, from my observation of actual events, would have defended me against a predator to the death.

I won't go through the vast animal kingdom, but it's been suggested that because all animals fight, some support the doctrine that warfare ought not be abolished amongst humans. It's been called Nietzscheism, Trotskyism and Prussianism. Essentially, for our basic understanding, it's militarism. Militarists in every nation are working hard to emphasize what they call a biological argument for war. They dwell on the cruelty and destruction that their ideas are a true picture of the life of animals and also of the nature of man. Pacifists weakly claim that no animal fights its own kind, but are refuted by the counter-punch that every animal fights its own kind. If we are to make an argument in support for militarism, it would not be done by using the example that the animals fight, so why not us? Conversely, if we are to make an argument for pacifism, the fact that all animals fight would not be worth the investigation for a logical comparison. Not all animals in fact fight, as we shall see.

Therefore, the question, "Why do animals fight?" need not relate to the human species as a generality and is a subject that cannot be broad-stroked in a semantic manner that relates to humans. But as we will later discuss, there appear to be some similarities, albeit in a somewhat remote sense. To make a statement that animals fight and therefore we should too may suggest that we hire a psychologist to assess the mind of the militarist. Don't get me wrong here; I'm not a pacifist, nor am I a militarist. My take is that if we are attacked by another nation, it's within our right to defend our sovereignty using military strength. The animal kingdom, especially animals in the wild, live under very different circumstances and fighting is not a militaristic bent or a sport.

Some animals will kill for what appears to be pleasure. A domestic cat will often play with a mouse until it is dead and not eat it. If the cat had not eaten in a while and was hungry, the mouse would most likely be eaten. If a man hunts and kills, morally, he should eat his game and not waste it. However, some hunters kill for the trophy. Animals are endowed with instincts that contradict what we might view as an illogical or inhumane behavior. Wild animals live in a different state of hunger than do domestic ones, and the hunt for food can appear to be quite gruesome. This is mostly what we see in nature documentaries, probably because humans have a curiosity about violence and death and nature moviemakers know this. In the wild, lions are more often seen basking in the sun or under the shade of a tree while their favorite meal is grazing in the background. Herds will sense when lions are out for lunch and will often ignore them wandering close to them when their bellies are full.

Often animals will kill in order to protect their food source. Some animals of the same species will fight to the death when there are too many of them and the food supply is scant. This is a struggle for existence and not a militaristic action. To understand why animals fight we must look at individual motives and fighting behaviors. To approach the subject from the myopic view of the entire animal kingdom to obtain a variety of miscellaneous information in support of the militaristic view of the human race would be archaic.

Therefore, let's examine a few behavioral traits of just a couple of species. Our closest genetic relatives from the animal kingdom are chimpanzees and bonobos. Chimpanzees are known to kill neighboring individuals. For years it's been thought that these vicious attacks were the result of some tribal warfare that they engaged in stemming from some form of hatred toward an individual or the neighboring group. A ten-year study of a chimp community in Uganda revealed definitive evidence that this behavior was to expand the group's territory, and not because the other group was ugly or had bad breath. Members of a larger community perpetrated eighteen fatal attacks on a smaller group. The area where eleven of these attacks occurred expanded the larger group's territory by twenty-two percent. After they used the new territory, the killing stopped and the group socialized and fed on their favorite fruits in their newly expanded region.

Bonobos, on the other hand, are more egalitarian and appear to substitute sex for aggression. While they engage in sex between males and females, they also do it with virtually every partner combination possible, including adolescents. They not only do it every which way but loose (and maybe even that way), but more often than any other primate. Since their sexual proclivity revolves around such diversity, their birth rate, or hit rate, is about the same as chimpanzees. Therefore, you might say that there's one characteristic bonobos share with humans—they have sex for pleasure and possibly entertainment as well as to propagate the species. As an experiment, I wonder if they would gather around a television screen to watch bonobo porn? Popcorn, anyone?

It's also well known that bonobos don't kill each other. This flies in the face of the militarist that entertains the idea that all animals kill. One study attributes this to affectional bonding between a mother and her offspring. It's believed that multiple consenting relationships are the key to their non-killing and peaceful behaviors. Remember the old Marlboro commercial where the smokers say, "I'd rather fight than switch"? Bonobos must be thinking, "I'd rather f--k than fight."

Bonobos are very sensitive, intelligent and imaginative. Their sensitivity is much greater than chimpanzees. During World War II, bombing in the city of Hellabrun, Germany caused all the bonobos there to die from fright generated by the noise of bombs going off, while the chimpanzees were unaffected. There's so much to say about bonobos. After this interesting research, I thought of changing the title of this book to *Why People Fight and Bonobos Don't*. But then I would have to undo almost everything I've written so far.

The similarities between the aggressive nature of animals and humans have its own chasm in ideologies and concepts amongst the psychologists and other intelligentsia. Among the arguments are that animals are aggressive and we cannot escape the legacy of our evolutionary ancestry. Sigmund Freud and Konrad Lorenz shared a belief that humans have a reservoir of natural and spontaneous animal aggression that periodically needs to be drained off. This can be done with exercise, competitive sports or hitting a punching bag before we explode into violence. Venting aggression is called catharsis, and is an idea stemming from Aristotle that we can purge negative emotion by watching tragic dramas. This belief is being held in some circles to this day. But many studies have revealed that engaging in such activities will make us more violent.

In 1986 behavioral scientists in Seville, Spain gathered together to discuss the root causes of human aggression. Their conclusions were that there is no scientific basis for the belief that humans are naturally aggressive and warlike. Comparing human behavior to that of the animals is a slippery slope. A stretch that compares animals to killers is to compare humans with meat-packing companies. Both species kill to eat, even if it involves killing carrot and potato plants. Another contrast that can be made about the animals based on the Seville study is that they often cooperate among themselves far more than what nature documentaries may portray. , Whether it's in nature or the environment of our cities, unless there is a respectable change within either one, it makes no sense to use an innate tendency for aggression over environmental change causing it.

Fighting amongst animals, provided they are not impaired with some disease such as rabies or brain disorders as in humans, does not contain some built-in behavioral or environmental basis to fight simply for the sake of fighting. Much like humans, fighting can be from a territorial threat, an expansion of territory to provide food for a growing group or a form of protectionism. This can be for a female, to protect young offspring or protection from being eaten for dinner, which doesn't apply too much to humans today. For animals it can include annoyances, as often seen on monkey island at metropolitan zoos, and for humans it can be found in the office environment, night-clubs and just about anywhere we congregate. It can also be the result of a totally imaginary threat. Humans basically fall within the same envelopes as animals, with an added feature that we think on a different level, incorporating a different knowledge set that complicates issues by orders of magnitude.

Logic, Reasoning Visual And Audio Input

8

Logic and reasoning point to that fighting may become so instilled within our minds from watching violence in games, movies, the news or knock-out videos that when an actual one erupts, the average American may not even stop to take notice anymore.

Although people fight for many different reasons, and despite the fact that we see violence on the nightly news over and over, each and every day, it must be noted that somewhere around 325 million people in the United States alone did not commit a homicide that day. If we take the most violent and dangerous countries in the world and rate them according to their number of 163 independent states, the safest is Iceland at 163, the least safe is Syria at number 1. With 325 million people not committing a homicide in the US, we are ranked 61, which puts us in the top one-third of the least safe countries in the world as of January 2017. It's actually safer to be in Uganda, Angola, Haiti or Mozambique than in America. The country I was born in, Canada, at 156 is even safer than Japan at 155.

Isn't it only logical that studies indicate that watching violence promotes violent behavior? Aren't we watching more and more blow-'em-up, shoot-'em-up movies and inspiring copycat violence through our news media? Hollywood has glamorized villains, and even taken two of our superheroes, Batman and Superman, and pitted them against each other! (Though it was all a misunderstanding and Superman, although it appears he was killed, is set up for a sequel.) The wholesome movies of the thirties and forties, even the fifties, are fewer and farther between. With the exception of romantic comedies, Hollywood seems bent on its continuation of violent movies.

Then there are the video games where combatants kill each other and are eliminated from the game. A task force has investigated whether there was an association between video games and violent behavior. The findings from the American Psychological Association show that these games increase aggression, but not enough to demonstrate that playing them leads to criminal behavior. They go on to explain that an accumulation of risk factors, such as antisocial behavior, depression, trouble at home, delinquency and academic problems, also play a role.

Take, for example, Adam Lanza, who was the perpetrator of the Sandy Hook Elementary shooting. It was discovered that he was obsessed with violent video games. Anyone that has children and is observant will see their child's behavior reflect a movie they have been engrossed in right after they have seen it. I know myself, when I was a kid, after seeing Walt Disney's *Davy Crockett* starring Fess Parker that I was obsessed with having a coonskin cap and a flintlock. Instead of a flintlock I had a Daisy air rifle that made a very real-sounding gunshot and I would go traipsing into the woods of Geauga Lake, Ohio, hoping I would run into a bear so I could kill it with my bare hands. After all, in the song of the movie, Davy Crockett had "kilt himself a bear when he was only three"!

Isn't it reasonable and logical to say that as a society, we change the next generation's direction with whatever exposure we present to it? Or, even more logically, doesn't each new generation lean toward its own path of preferred liking based on what they're exposed to? And yet here is another point of logic: If there's money to be made from the exploitation of popular celebrities, isn't the previous generation, with its years of contacts and expertise, going to promote whatever foul-mouthed, drug-taking obnoxious celebrity that may make them millions? And that whippersnapper of a celebrity gets the big head, thinks he's king of the earth and kicks the shit out of someone mainly from an elevated ego. I would even be tempted at that—so, I'm not taking sides here. There are many young celebrities that I admire and truly enjoy their creativity and obviously high intelligence. Unfortunately, the few that do get into trouble tarnish the reputation of others in their field. But the subject here is logic and reasoning as to why we become violent and fight.

If the list of safest to least safe countries were generated anywhere between 1875 and 1960, the US would be much closer to the safest than we are today. Violence today may not be attributed to video games or Hollywood's violent shoot-'em-up and blow-'em-up movies, but these are not helping, according to studies by researchers such as Ohio State University's Brad J. Bushman. He says, "…There certainly is a link between playing violent video games and violent criminal behavior, although it is not as strong as the link between playing violent video games and less serious aggressive behavior."

I like the line that politicians have commandeered from Obama's presidency, "Let me be clear." So, here it is …let me be clear, it's not the normal average person, youth or child that's going to be affected the most by watching violence. It's rather the person, youth or child that already has a propensity for violence that's going to be edged forward within that exposure to violence in any form. Studying a group of youth, even a large group, may not include that one-in-a-million youth that sooner or later may to be inspired, provoked or subconsciously urged into doing a violent and deplorable act. Note that I said "may" be inspired, and not that they *will be* inspired into doing a violent and deplorable act. That's just my opinion and I think it should be yours. I didn't make that line up. It's a line Chet Atkins, the world's greatest guitar player, often used.

But what if more and more people, especially our moldable youth, are exposed to violence in a sense that their pleasure centers feed back feelings of euphoria from watching fighting or actually fighting and winning? Could we someday be creating a generation where more and more youth develop some propensity for taking action toward the pleasure in winning a fight? And what about the ultimate horror when the reality of a violent act takes on a thrill that's greater than their vision for the continuation of their own life itself?

I was coming back from a client's business when I heard on the radio that a police officer was shot and killed that morning on a routine traffic stop. A second officer was also shot, but survived and was in the hospital. The shooter got away. A story like this goes out and lodges into the minds of certain people that now have empirical evidence that it's possible to avoid paying a ticket, or if there are warrants for their arrest, that they too have a chance to get away from the cops. All they have to do is shoot the police officer and then, as usual, go home for dinner—or hide out until the dust clears. Meanwhile, police officers become more and more trigger-nervous as they hear the same news. Case in point: someone was stopped for a routine traffic stop. While reaching for his certificate of insurance in his glove box, the officer thought he saw a gun and shot the innocent driver. A crowd gathered, which erupted in fighting in the street. Other people not involved casually drove away from the scene, went home to have their dinner as usual in front of their TV to watch more violence.

Logic and reasoning point to that fighting may become so instilled within our minds from watching violence in games, movies, the news or knock-out videos that when an actual one erupts, the average American may not even stop to take notice any more. People will calmly go about their business, bypassing the scuffle and peering into their cell phone, which is much more important to them—that is, unless they are bumped into and decide they've been "dissed." Society will have become comfortably numb to violence and killing, numb to another's pain, where the reality of life takes on a version of a crush, kill and destroy movie. The destruction of the human race could be a Hollywood movie where being exposed to violence for a few hundred years has turned the majority of humans into merciless, unfeeling psychopaths. They kill at every slight annoyance until there's no one left but one happy psychopath living on a mountain top in a Ted Kaczynski-type cabin.

Of course I'm exaggerating, but in only one lifetime, namely mine, I've seen violence increase on our streets, in our schools and in the home. In my youthful days in Ohio, no one could have even imagined a game called the "knock-out game." This is where someone walks up to a total stranger and punches them to knock them out while a friend records it. I would imagine that these young men then go home to watch it and laugh about it, maybe even while getting high.

We may not be in total control of our reactions to situations. In the study of animal behavior, it's known that animals consistently behave in certain ways to certain stimuli. Bears will react differently from deer when approached. Squirrels will play on wires strung between telephone poles, and skunks appear to be more business-like. There's a story about a turtle and a scorpion that depicts how we may not be in control of our emotions and actions as much as we might think.

The story goes like this: A scorpion wanted to cross a river when he met up with a turtle on its banks. The scorpion asked the turtle if he would allow him to ride on his back and take him across the river. The turtle responded, "Oh, I couldn't do that; you're a scorpion, and about halfway across the river, you will sting me and we will both die." The scorpion answered, "No, I wouldn't do that. All I want to do is go across the river." The turtle insisted that he would not do the deed and the scorpion continued to convince the turtle that he most certainly would not sting him. Finally the turtle agreed to take the scorpion across the river. Halfway across, the turtle felt the scorpion's stinger enter into his webbed foot. "You promised you wouldn't sting me! Look what you've done; now we will both die." To which the scorpion replied, "I can't help it. I'm a scorpion, that's what I do."

Fighting doesn't always include violence. When couples argue, it's usually the wife telling her female friend about the confrontation that will say something like, "We had a fight last night." If a male tells another male that he got into a fight, the first impression is that blood was drawn. When politicians fight, it's over issues and they mostly engage in civil discourse, although it can get pretty heated sometimes. There are many times that politicians have fought over flip-flopped issues that support the fluidity of beliefs but turned into a core of verbal exchanges over whether their opponent is stable. For years it was believed that secondhand smoke causes cancer leading to death. An article on a Forbes website stated, "A large-scale study found no clear link between secondhand smoke and lung cancer, undercutting the premise of years of litigation including a Florida case that yielded a $350 million settlement." For centuries, milk was good for you.

According to the Dairy Education Board, "Milk is a deadly poison." In the last four decades, it's vacillated back and forth. The same for eggs. One decade eggs are bad, the next decade eggs are good, then they're good, then bad. I believe that right now, eggs are good, but will they be when I'm eighty? Then the question will be, what the hell are those chickens eating?

One politician argued that if we send too many Marines to Guam, it will tip over. He also made an argument for the injustice against helium-filled balloons. His statement was, "Imagine a world without balloons." I'm certain that there are some people that now believe an island can tip over and that there exists a helium balloon crisis—somewhere. The idea that eating fat makes people fat was very popular for quite some time. How this got started, I don't know. The fact is that carbohydrates, proteins and fats are the building blocks of healthy nutrition. Eating fat doesn't make one fat. Eating lots makes one fat. It's like the comedian Carlos Mencia once said, "People get fat because they put more in this hole than what comes out of that hole." For a very long time in our American history, gay people were condemned for being themselves, and in some circles and according to some religious beliefs, they still are. I will say that in some circles, they will always be viewed as having behaviors that are not what would be viewed as normal. It's an observation of mine that I've never heard of a gay man beating up a straight man because he was straight. I have heard of lesbians attacking straight men for hitting on their girlfriends, but that's got an underlying reason besides a mere belief.

The Bible condemns "men who lie with men," and in Leviticus 20:13, "If a man has sexual intercourse with a male as one has sexual intercourse with a woman, the two of them have committed an abomination. They must be put to death; their blood guilt is on themselves." This verse supports the belief that homosexuality is bad. An opposing view is that in ancient history, sex was often viewed as a normal behavior. The term "homosexuality" was not a concept until after Christianity began to get a foothold over government policies like the Holy Roman Empire and Bible verses were turned into laws. Those who support homosexuality will cite the precept that the Levites were associated with the priesthood of Israel and were held to a higher standard and therefore, this abomination strictly applied to them. This is because it also states that eating shellfish and mixing certain clothing was too considered an abomination, and their argument adds that Jesus summed up God's commandments into two—love your neighbor as yourself and love God.

One near-death experiencer said that all that exists in the Universe is perfect. I happen to agree with this statement with one caveat, and it's the major factor that stands between us at peace and us fighting—our beliefs. It's not the varying beliefs that I'm questioning, but I still question unprovoked violence, whether it has any purpose. That may contradict the statement that everything is perfect, and if all is in fact perfect then I'm wrong. If this person's statement, and several others that have made that exhortation, are correct, that could only mean that fighting and conflict are part of a greater overarching condition of our existence and of the Universe. In short, opposing beliefs that trigger actions that can culminate in firing reward circuits in the brain are included by design.

Are there species on the planet that have overcome violence via some other reward path in their brains?

What separates the primates, the chimpanzee and the bonobo, from us is only one and a half percent of genetic sequencing. We are 98.5% the same and yet we cannot produce hybrid offspring. The DNA between species disallows interbreeding even amongst the closest of similarities. Each species comes with its own set of inborn skill sets from birth. From cockroaches to elephants to the great whales, all living things appear to have ingrained behaviors with preset knowledge according to each life form. The mighty oak tree grows to have its form from a little nut that drops onto the ground, while the caterpillar's destiny is programmed to morph from a crawling larva to spread wings and take to the sky. And humans may just have a predisposition that's in their DNA ladder from birth to experience anger, frustration, and irritability, as well as more positive attributes. Trying to find an anger circuit in the brain may be like trying to locate an underground lake by studying puddles in a field.

Some species, such as the bonobo, may not have anger genes and therefore are nonviolent. They may have rerouted the activation of their pleasure circuits through sexual activity rather than from the thrill of winning in battle. They may not be the only species that doesn't fight. I've never seen an angry caterpillar or have ever heard of one turn into a killer butterfly. That doesn't mean they don't get angry—maybe they do, who knows? It's my belief that all species come into this life with a complex character set that predetermines more than the number of digits at the ends of their extremities, the color of eyes and whether they have hair all over our bodies. It's the innate build program of genetic variation within the deoxyribonucleic acid (DNA) that determines what, and for that matter, who, we are. But what if we had control of some of this make-up prior to birth?

Although this may sound like a stretch to some, there are literally thousands of people who have had near-death experiences, claiming that we predetermine certain aspects of our existence. This might even include our propensities whether to kick someone's butt or leave him or her alone. Some cultures claim that we can reincarnate into another species. I found many references to humans reincarnating into animals, none of which made me feel solid about it. There were more convincing references to animals being of separate spirit genre. Therefore, I won't say that on the other side we can choose to reincarnate as animals or not. What I do aspire to is that our DNA, whether we have a say as to its structure prior to being born, is the being that we are destined to be. This also falls in line with knowledge and traits we as humans come into this world with and why baby birds instinctively know they were meant to fly.

We may very well fight because it's part of a complex set of instructions that makes up our physical structures and psychological inclinations. These DNA formulations, which are combined with what is thrown at us during the act of living with others and in our moments of solitude, set the triggers for how we react to what we perceive with our senses. Can we change these presets? The unequivocal answer is yes. Knowledge is power, and to have power over our genetic programming requires knowing that there is something that needs modifying or at least improving upon. We are dynamic learning machines, entities with the power of choice over what we do. Before we come here, we may in fact choose a set of traits and characteristics in order to present ourselves with the challenge to overcome them—albeit with some effort. This creates a condition whereby spiritual growth is the final result. To know, experience, and understand spiritual growth may just include re-experiencing a fight in our life's review.

Revenge

For you guys that harass using Twitter, I'd think twice about doing that. There may be copycat girl gangs out there that will literally clobber you into the ground.

There's a street culture that exists in which violence in some ways reflects the behaviors of animals fighting over their turf. The major difference is that animals will fight for turf, but revenge is less of a motive. It may appear that animals exact revenge, but for the most part, it appears to be a reactive act to displeasure. If enough time has passed, animals will not seek revenge, but will remember individuals that mistreated them.

The predator in the wild is respected and observed by those less fortunate to have the strength to defend themselves. They are always on the lookout for when the king of the turf may decide to attack for whatever reason, be it a cat/mouse or lion/gazelle thing. In the animal kingdom, this is usually for gaining territory or for an instant meal. In street culture it's not that much different, as territory can include the field in which money is made, and with money, pleasures can be bought. Rivals often try to encroach on territory for these rewards, in which violence often erupts. Again, winning the fight brings internal, personal rewards and possible external ones, and losing brings shame, defeat, anguish, dwelling on it and finally revenge.

Other high-risk conflicts where violence is perpetrated include abuse of family members, especially women and children, school peers and bullying, and general street-related offenses.

Changing macho behavior is a challenge many organizations are facing in inner cities, and with worthy success in some neighborhoods. It's not a simple task when the life of gang members includes debating whether some guys a couple of blocks away meant to insult you or not. Often it's whether you will make enough money for a meal or your next high. Mourning the loss of one of your "bros" and retaliating in their honor and wanting the cycle to stop means living in a perpetual dichotomy. This and being bored, having guns in your house and an ax to grind is therefore a sure recipe for violence.

One report from "Gang Ward," a Washington-based institute, reported that mentoring, recreational programs and job training have much more impact than areas that rely heavily on police enforcement. But these organizations eventually run out of money to operate while politicians turn a blind eye to their needs. In an article dated January 6, 2016 titled "Community Groups Can Make Up for Local Officials' Lack of Action on Gangs," Lynn Sharpe Underwood wrote, "Not only are San Diego's political and government services lacking a pointed, well-funded strategy on addressing the violence and poverty in our most under-served communities, but those with money are not willing to support efforts in those communities. There are a few private foundations that have taken on the mantle of care and they've been outstanding, but they're also stretched to the max."

Meanwhile, crimes occur like nine-year-old Tyshawn Lee's murder in Chicago when he was lured away from a playground. Two gang members approached him, took him into an alley a few blocks from his grandmother's home and shot him in the temple. The boy apparently tried to block the bullet, as an autopsy revealed that his thumb was partially severed by the bullet. The reason behind this senseless act was revenge for the killing of Corey Morgan's brother by a rival gang.

Tyshawn's father is allegedly part of the gang responsible for Corey's brother's death.

For you guys that harass using Twitter, I'd think twice about doing that. There may be copycat girl gangs out there that will literally clobber you into the ground. A group of girls attacked a man only named as E.C. for harassing his girlfriend on Twitter. The man was attacked as he was eating at an outdoor café. He was punched, kicked and kneed by seven girls before security guards stopped them. Did they overreact? Did the punishment fit the crime, if it was a crime in the first place? Revenge can blur common sense when anger overshadows flailing fists, feet and knees.

A pogrom is an organized massacre of a particular ethnic group. The Kielce pogrom was sparked by a small incident that was ripe for exploding into violence. Poland had been ethnically cleansed of Jews by Nazis during the war. In 1946, some two hundred Jews moved to Kielce. Many of them were former residents returning from concentration camps. Some Poles blamed the Jews for the German invasion of Poland, while others sided with Germany, blaming Jews for Germany's defeat. This was a catch-22 for Jews in Poland.

A prime example of how revenge can take on an uncalmable momentum of its own occurred right after World War II. On July 4, 1946, in the city of Kielce, Poland, an eight-year-old boy, Henryk Blaszczyk, claimed he was kidnapped by Jews and held for two days. That morning, while his father was taking him to the police station, they passed an apartment house at 7 Planty Street, where Henryk pointed at a man claiming he had imprisoned him in that house. Henryk repeated his story at the police station and more than a dozen men were dispatched to the house on Planty Street.

By ten o'clock the same morning, the police had publicized the rumors of the kidnapping by announcing that they were planning to search for bodies of Polish children. A crowd gathered and a confrontation ensued. This was between police and officers of the Ministry of Public Security of Poland, who were called on the suspicion that there was a Jewish provocation to stir up unrest. It wasn't long before other local state and the military sent about one hundred soldiers and five officers there. The soldiers had not been told anything about the incident, but heard rumors from people on the street. People began pelting the house with rocks. The police and soldiers then broke into the house and found nothing of importance, but Jewish residents were ordered to surrender all their weapons even though they had permits for them. Shooting erupted and soon there were dead bodies.

After these initial killings, more Jews were forced outside by soldiers where they were attacked by civilians. By noon, two hours later, a large group, estimated between six hundred and a thousand workers from a nearby steel mill, had come to the aid of the townspeople armed with steel rods and clubs. It's estimated that twenty Jews were brutally beaten to death while a unit of police did nothing to prevent the carnage. Some of them joined in the looting of the three-story apartment house.

Nine Jews were shot, two were killed with bayonets and the rest were beaten and stoned to death. They also killed a nurse and two Jews who did not live at the Planty Street apartment. Regina Fisz and her three-week-old son Abram were also killed.

The event eventually ended around three p.m., but did not stop there. Wounded Jews were beaten and robbed by soldiers on their way to hospitals. Trains passing through Kielce's main railway station were searched for Jews, resulting in at least two being shot and as many as thirty more murders were reported over the following several months.

Henryk remained silent about the incident until 1998, when it was revealed in an interview to a Polish journalist that he had made the story up about being kidnapped. He maintained that his father knew where he actually was and a conspiracy exists to this day.

At the end of the war, Winston Churchill established what was called the "Jewish Brigade." Churchill commented, "It seemed to me indeed appropriate that a special unit of the race which has suffered indescribable treatment from the Nazis should be represented in a distinct formation among the forces gathering for their final overthrow." They were called Din squads, which is Hebrew for "revenge." Over six thousand men volunteered for this unit. One anonymous member of the revenge squad elaborated, "When the bastards realized we were Jews, you could almost smell the funk. I did take a great deal of pleasure in making them kneel and pointing my gun at them. I made more than one member of the master race mess his pants with fright."

Aleksander Laak was the last person killed by the revenge squad.

Laak ran the Jagala concentration camp in Estonia, where over one hundred thousand people had been murdered. He had fled to Canada and must have thought he was safe there fifteen years after the war ended, but in 1960 the revenge squad found him and hanged him. As one member, named Zeer Keren, is quoted, "We were quite happy to do to the Nazis what they had done to the Jews. I strangled one myself once … it took three to four minutes."

But what does revenge comprise both psychologically and physically, and what has the science of revenge revealed? When Swiss researchers of Empirical Research in Economics at the University of Zurich in Switzerland studied the brains of people who had recently been wronged in a money exchanging game they gave to them in the lab, they discovered a rush of neural activity in the dorsal striatum. Interestingly, this is the portion of the brain that processes rewards, enjoyment or satisfaction. They also discovered that this part of the brain lit up according to how much punishment the subject chose to mete out upon the adversary who wronged them. The more it lit up, the greater the retaliatory action and vice versa. Sweet revenge may be just that, but now we know why it's sweet. It may not be tit for tat, but how we perceive the punishment for some wrongdoing. Ernst Fehr, director of the institute, stated, "The person would feel even worse if the cheater does not get her or his just punishment." Their deduction was that meting out altruistic punishment might be the glue that holds societies together.

They forgot one thing, and that's perception. Their idea holds that, "Cooperation among strangers breaks down in experiments if altruistic punishment is ruled out. Cooperation flourishes if punishment of defectors is possible." Cooperation is one thing; however, there's a hitch in the get-along, and that's where revenge is based on a perceived wrong or the act of meting out an over-reactive judgment. In the Kielce case, the perception was wrong and over reaction was executed based on hearsay. In either situation, whether it was illogically perceived or over reaction, the result in the dorsal striatum is the same, at least until the facts are realized.

In a similar way that the amygdala regulates emotions and the nucleus accumbens releases dopamine that innervates the hypothalamus that informs of the presence of rewards, this revenge circuit also stimulates pleasure, whether it's rational or not. We can therefore conclude that whether we fight over some superfluous reason and win, or mete out revenge onto someone that deserves it or not, our brains still put us in happy mode.

Fighting The Good Fight

10

What started out as a good fight against polytheists over a belief that there was only one God has led to over two thousand years of hatred between people with a common ancestry and even a common religious origin.

I've mentioned that we can't be wrong in our beliefs. There's also the fact that not all beliefs agree in their base doctrines, and even down to the most miniscule notions about certain things fall into the same category. What we believe governs us in everything we do and everything we think. Most people on the planet perceive themselves as being good, moral and benevolent—at least somewhat. Some are just scoundrels, but I'm sure very few of them actually believe they are.

We are, for the most part, good people. That is, until we begin comparing beliefs. Liberals may believe conservatives want to throw Grandma over a cliff strapped to her wheelchair, and conservatives may believe liberals don't know how to tell the truth. Most Christians believe that Muslims can't get to heaven because they don't believe in

Jesus, and Muslims (radical ones) believe in a jihad, or fight against everyone that's not a Muslim. It's not too far from the song "Merry Minuet" by The Kingston Trio: "The French hate the Germans, the Germans hate the Poles, Italians hate Yugoslavs, South Africans hate the Dutch. And I don't like anybody very much!"

People fight over the darndest things. And I can say that, because I have my own set of beliefs that I will fight (only verbally) for. At nearly seventy, I would have a difficult time fighting my way out of a wet paper bag, but as we get older, we tend to settle into our grooves and some of us become curmudgeonly as we get older. That's not to say I'm bad-tempered, but I quickly dismiss beliefs that I know from experience are way out of whack from reality, or at least my perception of reality. When someone starts to blurt out that there's no God, or that there have never been any clear pictures of a UFO, that's when I may begin to shoot daggers out of my eyes. These little daggers are projected out in the direction of the myopic-thinking person that's most likely never took more than a few minutes looking into the subjects they don't believe in. If they wish to engage in dialogue and not spew out a diatribe of verbal diarrhea, I'll discuss my beliefs with them. I believe in an intelligence that started everything and I videotaped a UFO that I analyzed with histograms, color hues and several other photographic analysis tools. What's more, since I'm constantly scanning the sky, I've seen them several times. One just has to keep it up and sooner or later, you too will see one. I also believe we can have consciousness outside our bodies, which to me means that we don't die; we merely pop out of this physical container and become a conscious being less a physical form.

There are many people that will staunchly fight, whether with words, fists, clubs and even guns over the simplest and mundane of beliefs. However, there are a couple of general belief categories that are best left alone when encountering such a person—politics and religion. These subjects invoke a behavior in people that hold the belief that they are fighting the good fight. Christians will quote First Timothy 6:12, "Fight the good fight of the faith. Take hold of the eternal life to which you were called and about which you made the good confession in the presence of many witnesses." Other groups are fighting the good fight against cancer, women's issues, black lives matter, and the Winnipeg

General Strike of 1919 where 25,000 workers gathered, street cars were tipped over, mounted police charged down Main Street and it became known as "Bloody Saturday." It was initially called "fighting the good fight." Good fights can quickly turn into bad fights.

People of the same ilk usually back good fights. The okay to fight a good fight may be spurned on by people of power, such as politicians, people of noble intent such as religious leaders and respected good talkers. They may believe they have the blessings of God as written in the Bible, the Quran, the Shrimad Bhagavad Gita, the Tripitaka, the Guru Granth Sahib and even the Kitab-I-Aqdas. There's probably no better example of a good fight than a religious or holy war. However, "religious war" is a modern term, since the very concept of religion is a recent invention in the English language. The term "religion" was translated from many older terms, meaning worship rather than a set of beliefs. Hebrew has no direct equivalent for the word religion, and the Japanese had no word for religion until American warships off its coast in 1853 forced them to sign treaties demanding freedom of religion where the Japanese had to contend with the idea.

According to Steven Pinker, one of the world's leading authorities on the mind, religion accounts for only thirteen out of one hundred of the world's worst atrocities in human history. Charles Phillips and Alan Axelrod in their *Encyclopedia of Wars* state that before the 17th century, wars were explained through the lens of religion. After that time, they were explained as a way to further sovereign interests. The underlying reasons fare more under the auspices of prejudice, envy, coercion and a sense of injustice. Some state that only 7% of 1,763 wars in their study originated with religious motivations.

Even the portrayal of the religious differences between Catholics in Ireland and British Protestants was in fact more ethnic and nationalistic, rather than religious, in nature. The same could not be said of those who fought in the name of God during the Crusades. These were a series of military campaigns from the 11th through the 13th centuries against the Muslim conquests of Europe. The original purpose was to recapture Jerusalem and the Holy Land from the Muslims. In 1095, Pope Urban II raised the level of war from "just war" to "holy war." In the quest for religious liberation from the Muslims, political conflicts also arose, such as the Aragonese Crusade declared by Pope Martin IV against King Aragon of Sicily. Historian H. J. Chaytor described the Aragonese Crusade as "perhaps the most unjust, unnecessary and calamitous enterprise ever undertaken by the Capetian monarchy." And most likely all in the name of "the good fight."

Today, the Israeli-Palestinian conflict appears to be over religion. Abraham is given a high position of respect in Judaism and Islam. He lived from around 1800 BCE to around 1600 BCE—a couple of hundred years. Originally it's believed that these two religious factions separated over which brother Abraham was to sacrifice, Ismail or Isaac, but God instructed Abraham to do a goat instead. The Jews say it was Isaac who was to be sacrificed and the Muslims believe it was Ismail. Was the split between these people over two brothers and a goat, or might it have been more serious?

Some thousand years later, in 630 AD, Mohammed was fighting to take over Mecca from polytheists when it was rumored that the Jews of Banu Qurayza were conspiring with the Meccans. This didn't sit well with Mohammed, although it was also rumored that it was he that started the rumors in the first place. The alleged conspirators were given a choice to be judged under Muslim or Jewish laws. Sa'd ibn Mu'adh was appointed as their judge, whom they believed would be fair since he was a Jew, but had converted to Islam. Unfortunately, Sa'd ordered the execution of 600 to 900 men by cutting off their heads. While some Muslim scholars reject the incident, many Jewish accounts are claimed to have embellished the facts. And that, I believe, was the real beginning of the Israeli-Palestinian conflict that's been ongoing for 2,645 years and counting.

What started out as a good fight against polytheists over a belief that there was only one God has led to over two thousand years of hatred between people with a common ancestry and even a common religious origin. These facts are all but forgotten. All that is remembered are the recent acts of violence perpetrated against the other over territory, freedoms and fear of loss. Remember sweet revenge?

In Christianity, fighting the good fight today is being preached as a weapon against spiritual hosts of wickedness. It's touted as a never-ending struggle against evil. It's not a battle against another military faction; it's a battle against Satan. I taught the Bible for nearly a decade in the Deep South and at that time, I believed every word in it.

I nearly got beat up by two preachers that disagreed with what I had learned in the scriptures. I don't think that would have been a "good fight"—two against one! Their fists were clenched and their faces were fire-engine red. I hightailed it back to my car, not looking back to see if they were running after me. What would have I told my wife then? "Honey, I got my ass kicked for trying to explain my beliefs in the Bible to these two other Bible guys that had a different set of beliefs." I thought to myself, "What the hell am I trying to do here? These people don't want dialogue; they just want me to convert to their way of thinking." However, isn't that just what I was doing too? The only difference was that I wasn't getting angry and they were. (There's also a difference between a fight and an old-fashioned beating.)

Common sense is where keeping the faith and not getting your ass kicked makes a line of demarcation. I went away wondering why these two men of faith, these two leaders in their Christian church, would want to resort to fighting over nothing more than a belief.

One explanation might be that they simply didn't want anyone telling them that they were wrong. There may be a more deep-seated reason why we hang onto our beliefs despite evidence to the contrary, and that's what psychologists call cognitive dissonance. This is when we are presented with two opposing views or ideas about a subject. Leon Festinger coined the term in 1954 to describe a feeling of psychological discomfort produced by two thoughts that don't agree with each other. It's the smoker that knows that smoking is not good for their health and will support the conflicting knowledge saying that it's not as bad as everyone says. It's rationalization or even denial of facts when faced with cognitive dissonance. Over a period of time, these rationalizations and denial of facts form a bias for one conflicting idea over another, even if the one chosen is shown to be incorrect. The biased mind will look for more support for a particular belief and reinforce it until it becomes like the old Marlboro commercial mentioned in chapter seven, where the actor says, "I'd rather fight than switch."

Vexen Crabtree, a Satanist, is quoted as saying, "Something about religious beliefs leads to violent intolerance. I think it is this: Some will defend with violence and aggression beliefs that they can't defend with evidence." This may be true of some people, therefore making him partially correct. On the other hand, I believe in a Creator and the concept of good and that religion in general is good. That's not evidence; it's only my opinion. One thing that drives some people away from religion is when it's associated with violent fanaticism. People fighting in the name of their religion, the good fight, that are causing pain, suffering and bloodshed may turn many away from all religion in general.

The Pew Research Center showed that Americans who believed in God dropped from 71% to 63% between 2007 and 2015. The greatest decline in religious belief was with millennials. The report goes on to reveal that there is a polarization in religiosity between the nonbelievers and those with a religion becoming more devout. These escalating opposing beliefs may set the stage for more good fights against things like abortion, and countered good fights from the LGBT community.

Unprovoked Aggression

A surprising result based on a lexical decision task to determine the state of thought effects revealed that participants who responded faster to "happy" words after viewing violent photos were significantly more likely to engage in unprovoked aggression.

Have you ever just looked at a total stranger and said or thought something derogatory about them? Without even talking to that person, or finding out anything about them, you formed an opinion based on a visual input, a first, first impression. I certainly have. In fact, being a business owner, it's one of my first lines of defense as to whether I want to do further business with any person. If a new client comes in looking homeless and smelling like the north end of a southbound mule, I form an immediate opinion.

Fortunately I'm not an aggressive type, and may even try to help that person in any way I can. I've actually had a client come to me for some product development that was homeless. He slept in a small compact and I thought of giving him one of our company vans just so he could stretch out a bit at night. I didn't do it, and still feel some form of guilt for even thinking that and never following through. I will often stop my car to offer a homeless person a twenty-dollar bill just because I know what it's like living on the street. I did this for nearly a year when I was nineteen years old, and believe me, it wasn't fun. I write about this episode in my life in *Where's My Mom and Dad?*

On the flip side, I was coming to my office about two weeks ago when I saw a poor guy carrying what looked like everything he owned in a large burlap sack tied on his back with white packing string. His clothes were filthy and tattered, and his hair stuck out like he had been sitting on a Van de Graaff generator. I slowed down, looking at him as I reached into my pocket for at least a twenty, when we locked eyes. We had made a connection. Mine was of compassion for another human being, while he raised his hand with his arm outstretched and gave me the finger—the middle one! I must not have made a positive first impression with this guy. I thought about it for a while, and the only thing I could think of was that he was black and I was just another angry honky staring at him. I kept driving out of fear that if I stopped my van and got out of its protective shell, this seventy-year-old white guy was going to get a serious bruising.

Looking at someone and taking an aggressive stance is different from an act of unprovoked aggression. I never stayed very long in any high school because my dad was always looking for greener pastures and we moved a lot. We had moved to Mesa, Arizona from Geauga Lake, Ohio, and after I had been in that new school for about a month, I had made literally no friends. One lunch hour, I was walking on the campus when one of four chubby ruffians rammed his elbow into my chest, nearly knocking me down. I regained some composure, thinking they must have mistaken me for someone much uglier. The ordeal might have escalated into a one-sided brawl when, fortunately, one of them told me to just get the hell away before I get hurt … which is exactly what I did. My only thought then was, "Boy, what a bunch of psychos in this school." In reality I wasn't too far off, at least maybe not for this particular aggressor.

We discussed some aspects of psychopathic behavior in chapter two. As it was mentioned, psychopathy is a matter of degree, and in its mildest forms the psychopath can be interchangeable with the sociopath. Both are characterized as possessing emotional and interpersonal traits that include lack of remorse, manipulativeness, absence of empathy, superficial charm and so on. Needless to say, the chubby bully psycho had no charm at all. A second tier of psychopathy can include substance abuse, high sensation-seeking, irresponsibility, lack of concern or plans for the future, and early life behavioral problems. Perhaps the most notable is the stunning lack of empathy and lack of remorse.

Historically, psychopathy has been at the root of some of the some of the most violent, aggressive, gratuitous and sadistic of crimes. According to Miller & Lynam, Parrot & Seichner, Reidy, Zeichner, Miller, & Martinez, all of whom were involved in laboratory-based research utilizing subclinical, non-forensic populations, it has been repeatedly confirmed that psychopathy predicts aggression.

The University of Georgia did a study of unprovoked aggression using one hundred thirty-seven men to determine the effects of psychopathic traits and sadism. Why they didn't use any women is not indicated in their study. A surprising result based on a lexical decision task to determine the state of thought effects revealed that participants who responded faster to "happy" words after viewing violent photos were significantly more likely to engage in unprovoked aggression. The implication, at least in men, demonstrated that unprovoked violence may be more of a situational motivation rather than an impulsive one. In addition, a faster response to happiness words after viewing violent imagery would indicate that pleasure was derived from viewing such content. They hypothesized that psychopathy would predict higher probability of unprovoked aggression. This resembles a bit the pleasure attained from non-schizophrenics after winning a bloody fight and going out to look for another one.

In the Reidy, Zeichner, Miller and Martinez study (2008), participants were categorized as unprovoked, retaliatory and non-aggressors contingent on their responses to the experiment. The experiment involved giving electrical shocks to an opposing individual. The high psychopathy participants were 60% more likely to be unprovoked aggressors than their low-psychopathy counterparts. Also, the non-aggressor aggressed only after provocation.

The final conclusion was that highly psychopathic individuals are more likely to engage in violence of greater severity and do it more often. They also state that this data is consistent with previous research that says exactly the same thing. It's been very interesting reading not only this ninety-five page report, but several others to find all this out, but disappointing to surmise that our government paid lots of money to learn what they already knew. Maybe government-funded researchers, although not psychotic, may be a bit neurotic. Then again, they may merely have had a Mercedes payment coming up and decided, "Let's do an easy study to find out what we already know."

To summarize, we can't get out of the person that we are. Our first impressions are based on our beliefs and perceptions, and there's nothing we can do about it. Psychopaths are like the scorpion; they merely do what they do because of what they are. It may be the responsibility of society to identify who is really nuts and who isn't, but the way our justice system is set up, one can't incarcerate someone until after they have committed a crime. The psychopath is left to his devices to stew and brew until he commits an act of unprovoked, sometimes diabolical aggression. Only then do we call them monsters.

Fighting Comes In Waves

12

After the US Civil War, a wave of violence swept across the country. This peaked around 1870. There was quiet within the US borders throughout WWI, when civil discord erupted again around 1920 with race riots, workers' strikes and a surge of anti-Communist feelings. In the 1970's unrest crested again when students began to demonstrate against "the man," overshadowed with political assassinations and homegrown terrorism.

I couldn't write a book on why people fight without including what I erroneously thought Dennis Prager's book was about, but from a different perspective. War means different things to different people. For my aunt, it was the reason for the loss of my uncle's left leg in Sicily. As for my uncle, he would only talk about it for a certain amount of time before I got the feeling he wanted to change the subject. My best friend from high school told me that fighting in Vietnam was the most exciting time of his life. He wished he could go back, even though he still has shrapnel in his body and received a Purple Heart medal while losing eight of his buddies in one direct hit. My son says he's glad he went to Afghanistan, and that he really doesn't wish to go back, but would go without hesitation if asked to.

Much of what I've researched about war has been from university research papers and books describing what the nature of war is all about. Although these writers claim that their purpose is different or unique, the contents of their pages could be interchanged and the reader would not know the difference. Phrases like, "weakly institutionalized nation states," "rebel fighters," "principles of legitimacy" and so on did not leave a mark in my neurological record grooves as to the core reason for war. It left me still wondering why the study of war and the verbose treatise on the subject is made to look so complex. Yes, I agree that differences in social, economic, political, ethnic, religious, etc. views are complex and provide varying reasons leaders might wish to escalate these differences into killing each other. However, there must be a common denominator that can encompass some baseline as to why wars have been recycling themselves since the beginning of human history.

A workshop was conducted in Knoxville Tennessee on the evolution of war, hosted by the University of Tennessee's National Institute for Mathematical and Biological Synthesis to develop mathematical and biological approaches to understanding complex systems. Their reasoning for believing their ideas would be more informatory was because of better definitions than what was done in the past; theories are more nuanced and more abundant evidence is available.

They suggest that evolutionary theory allows for insight into ancient origins of war and their causes. If you've read my previous books, you know that I like to look at the humorous side of things. One sentence in the results of their study states, "While war takes many forms—gang violence, terrorism, insurgency, rebellion, civil war, interstate war—an important commonality is that they are fought, and led, by human beings." Can I be a bit satirical by saying, "I now have the answer to how to stop all war—get rid of human beings!" … I just couldn't help that.

I understood their meaning. Although their conclusion pointed to a better understanding of when and why people fight from an evolutionary perspective, it left me rather hollow. Maybe for the same reason that we're able to statistically examine past conflicts, we still don't have an answer as to how to prevent them and maybe never will. As one conflict is ending and everyone cheers in the streets, another appears to be brewing on the horizon—somewhere. That may be why we say that history repeats itself. It's like I've written before, the human race is here for the experience—after we experience war, we want peace—after we've experienced peace for a while, we get bored and want war—and on and on.

Let's look at just the past couple of hundred of years. After the US Civil War, a wave of violence swept across the country. This peaked around 1870. There was quiet within the US borders throughout WWI, when civil discord erupted again around 1920 with race riots, workers' strikes and a surge of anti-Communist feelings. In the 1970's unrest crested again when students began to demonstrate against "the man," overshadowed with political assassinations and homegrown terrorism.

Peter Turchin, a professor of population dynamics at the University of Connecticut, says that political instability that occurs at approximately every fifty years is not a coincidence. He has taken a mathematical technique that for the past fifteen years has allowed him to track and predict predator/prey cycles in the wild and apply them to humans. His math predicts that a peak in violence should occur around 2020. He says that the violence may equal that of the 1970's and hopes it won't be as bad as the 1870's. He's applied scientific methods to history in order to model broad social forces that shape all human societies. This approach is to show that history is much more than simply one damn thing after another, as the British historian Arnold Toynbee once noted.

Turchin and his allies say that we are in a position to revisit general laws thanks to things like non-linear mathematics and other techniques that allow for gathering and analyzing huge amounts of data. It's time to abandon the examination of a few sample cases and assert generalizations from these. Turchin's father, a computer scientist from Russia, was exiled for his dissident writings about the origins of totalitarianism and moved to the United States near the end of the seventies. He names his approach "cliodynamics" after Clio, the Greek muse of history. His algorithms aren't a search for patterns, but are a systematic collection of centuries, even millennia of data and how their mathematical variables interact. The four main variables are population numbers, social structure, state strength and political instability. Then each variable is measured in several different ways. It's cleverly complicated, but drawing from all sources, their approach then can find associated archives and studies to plot these proxies over time and look for trends to future events.

There are two interacting cycles that fit patterns of instability from the fifth century BC onwards. These include the transition of the Roman Empire and even patterns in ancient Egypt, China and Russia. These are longer cycles they call secular cycles that occur over two to three centuries. Superimposed over that secular trend are shorter cycles that occur roughly every two generations. He calls these father-and-son cycles. Grandpa had responded violently to some perceived social injustice. Dad witnessed it or remembers the useless violence and abstains. The son is unhappy about something, anything, and needs to voice his "change" muscles and it starts again. It's like a forest fire that ignites, and then burns out until there's no more fuel. Then, enough fuel grows when the fire is lit again.

These algorithms have been applied to how religions grow. The predictions of his mathematics were massaged to parallel the growth of Islam, and then accurately describe the expansion of Christianity and Mormonism. Other researchers say that cliodynamics is a suitable predictor of some aspects of human behavior as it relates to war and violence, but when it comes to predicting more unique events, such as the biography of noted individuals, the conventional narrative-based evidence works better. Herbert Gintis, a retired economist at the University of Massachusetts Amherst, believes that cliodynamics may offer policy-makers valuable lessons that might stave off trouble.

This peace/unrest cycle has been historically repeated over and over and may be endless. If Turchin's predictions are correct about 2020, the United States should watch for an increase in tightly-knit groups whose activities have a threatening posture, but their belief is that they will attain certain great rewards. Whether these great rewards are worth the fight may not even matter to the instigators, who may not realize that they are only flexing their "want" muscles. I don't mean to be a skeptic over positive changes that have come about from conflicts, but too many conflicts have killed people and disrupted lives over ideologies that were not commensurate with the damage they caused.

For example, Hitler's master race didn't make it, yet, for a mere ideology, millions were killed. Capitalism has sprung up all over China while Chairman Mao lies quietly in his casket after millions more were killed. His "Great Leap Forward" aimed at mass mobilization of labor to improve agricultural and industrial production resulted in a mass decline in harvests that led to famine and the deaths of approximately 1.5 million people. Before his death, he tried rebuilding bridges with the United States, Japan and Europe, realizing he might have screwed up. Joseph Stalin was another charismatic leader that so many believed had his head up his sphincter. His country's death toll from famine is estimated between five and ten million people. Millions more were executed because of their opposing views.

Joseph Stalin certainly led an interesting life, and I recommend looking him up. In a controversial poll taken in 2006, it was stated that more than 35% of Russians would vote for him if he were alive today. Fewer than 33% viewed him as a murderous tyrant, and in a 2007 poll, 50% of respondents aged from sixteen to nineteen said Stalin was a wise leader.

My personal conclusion for the reason for war is not much different from two neighbors fighting over another's dog barking or that one's tree is hanging over the other's car and dripping sap all over it. It's not much different from two workers doing the same job squabbling over one getting ten cents more per hour. It's also akin to a robber breaking into a house to steal the stuff. It's not complicated; it's just on a much larger and more complicated scale. We don't appear to get wiser over the centuries. The next chapter may reveal a reason for that.

Nations of the world elect leaders, and these leaders most often must comply with the collective mindsets of what the people they are leading want most. In many cases, it's the other way around. The people are so enamored with the charisma of their leader that they will follow him right over a cliff. Wars are a macro rendition of micro conflicts, whether they are two four-year-old neighbors fighting over a little red wagon or gang warfare where the stakes are more serious.

War is the epitome of serious conflict, and as long as we exhibit the traits encoded in our human DNA, we will continue to fall prey to our ingrained instincts.

Human Experience Is Only About Seventy Years

13

Memories are short and legends of past generations that have endured to this day are few. History gets forgotten and often simply rewritten, where archeologists may be so proud as to believe their finding of every scrap of cuneiform as true.

A generation comes and a generation goes. Each generation is here for a fleeting moment within human history. We come into existence with no knowledge, no experience, except that with which we were genetically encoded. From all of human history, we in fact only have the experience of somewhere around seventy years. That's because we only live around seventy years on average. It's like the boss talking about one of his employees and says, "When I hired him, he said he had twenty years of experience. From what I see, he's actually only got one year of experience twenty times." Think about that for a moment and see if I make a modicum of sense. Our ancestors have been here for some six million years. Written human history is only about six thousand years old. Do we engage in fighting with each other because we haven't learned enough not to? What's more, do we in fact have a mere seventy years of experience 85,714 times? Or, at best, seventy years of experience based on six thousand years of written history at 85.7 times? No matter how one slices it, it's still only around seventy years of experience.

Let's dissect that statement a bit more. Let's say the smartest man in the world read every book he could within his lifetime, watched all the educational videos he could within his lifetime, took every college and university subject he possibly had time for, and slept only six hours per day. How much knowledge could he have packed away? What's more, even if he became president of the most powerful country in the world, could he sway the people that have much less knowledge than him? What about the masses of people on the planet that only learned one-tenth of what he knew? Wouldn't the collective knowledge only add up to a total of around seventy years of learning? In the fields of psychology, astronomy, history and every discipline taught, aren't we still isolated by what each individual can absorb within a lifetime anyway? As a human species, we don't live long enough to mature into such wisdom that we can solve our most pressing problems. It seems that every generation is faced with the same ones over and over. These include injustice, aggression, imposition, disagreement, tyranny and other factors that cause turmoil.

One of the most prolific savants that has ever been recorded finished his high school curriculum at the age of fourteen. When he was eighteen, he was doing the payroll for a company that had 160 people and finished the task in only two hours with no calculator. He was able to remember things as young as sixteen months old. He would read a book, and then place it upside down on a shelf to indicate that he had read it. It would take him about an hour to read an average book and remember nearly every word. It's been written about him that he could remember the contents of around 12,000 books. With all that memory, Kim Peek's IQ was only 87, which is below average. My point here is that even if someone were to gather all the information available as data, would they have that other trait of common sense or wisdom to adapt that knowledge into a form that could change the world for the better?

Sure, there have been many people that have improved upon our society. Steve Jobs certainly changed the world with his vision, but could he have stopped wars? Socrates taught a method of self-inquiry, the power of integrity and encouraged people to be honest, but war raged on. Jesus Christ, a spiritual teacher and the inspiration for Christianity, inspired millions, but war raged on. The human race today can be characterized as having been here for a very long time and yet possessing a very short amount of practical experience on how to bring about lasting peace on the planet.

All wars have the same basic characteristics, and these can be boiled down to differences in thought. We can only learn so much within even the collective experience of each generation; it's what we've learned that culminate into our thoughts and it's the types of thoughts that are at the root of the many reasons why we fight.

From an altruistic point of view, fighting can be observed like we're all a bunch of little kids fighting over toys in our human sandbox. From my point of view, it could be that we just can't get along because we haven't had enough time to wise up from previous bloodshed. Or, could it be that the plan for us comes from a divine source that designed it that way for us to learn something with each generation? I can relate with the view that everything is perfect in the sense that everything that happens has meaning and purpose, even war. What has history taught us and who's in charge to use that knowledge? Are we just a bunch of fifty to seventy-year-old children running the show?

According to Biblical history, we used to live longer, much longer. The Bible's historical record of the age of the patriarchs was around nine hundred years prior to the great flood. According to the Bible, Jared lived nine hundred sixty-two years and Methuselah was nine hundred sixty-nine when he died. After the account of the flood, the age of recorded patriarchs dropped dramatically to less than one hundred twenty years and has remained there to this day.

But, if people lived nine hundred years, where are their bones? Dr. Jack Cuozzo makes a compelling argument that the many skulls of Neanderthals that have been found are in fact modern, intelligent humans that lived to that ripe old age. His argument is that many of the skulls found of Neanderthals grew at a rate that was much slower than present-day skulls because of their long life, and is why they are shaped differently. In order to support the theory of evolution, anthropologists modified Neanderthal skulls to look more ape-like rather than human. Dr. Jack Cuozzo witnessed an anthropologist actually cutting off the chin of a Neanderthal jawbone because apes don't have chins and this would contradict the theory of evolution. His findings and exposé of skull tampering by anthropologists is part of his evidence in his theory supporting the Bible's account of humans living hundreds of years.

Dr. Cuozzo had a computer model of skull growth based on skull X-rays done of university graduates that were taken at yearly intervals until they were in their eighties. The model then projected further bone growth based on that rate of growth; in other words, what a human skull would look like if that person lived to five hundred years. He speculates that Noah looked pretty grotesque according to our standards of handsome. In essence, he would look very much like a Neanderthal.

According to the bone growth characteristics, the brow moves forward, the rear of the head elongates rearward and the chin recedes because of the teeth and cheeks moving forward. A Neanderthal male skull was found in France buried in a cave in the town of La Chapelle-aux-Saints in 1908 that had these precise characteristics. It's also been confirmed that according to examination of just the skulls, orthodontists that examined these skulls and were not told they were Neanderthals speculated that these were of people that were very large and never suspected they were Neanderthals.

Depictions of Neanderthals showing hair all over their bodies may erroneously be artist representations requested by anthropologists. One researcher stated that since there were few tools found that were used for the secondary process of animal skins necessary to produce clothing that would protect the Neanderthal from the bitter cold, they must have been furry. That presupposes that the weather was in fact cold. That also ignores the fact that many warm-climate animals have been found trapped in muck and ice above the Arctic Circle during some fast-acting cold wave that entombed them for centuries. These animals and Neanderthals existed in the same time period. It must have been warm that far above the Arctic Circle, since buttercups were found in their stomachs. Since it's not known what actually caused the Neanderthals to vanish, maybe it was simply because they went from nine hundred years old to a youthful one hundred twenty and never really disappeared—they only got younger and prettier, like us.

Living to hundreds of years might provide answers to many of the highly advanced artifacts that have been found from ancient times. If ancients lived longer, could they have developed techniques for building structures that we don't have the experience to replicate because we haven't had enough time to think about it?

Evidence of advanced technology from ancient civilizations has been uncovered that lends credibility to the intelligence of ancient peoples. One finding was of a drill bit that John Buchanan, Esquire, presented to the Society of Antiquities of Scotland on December 13, 1852. The drill bit was embedded in coal that was about seven feet thick. Geologists estimated the coal formed several hundreds of millions of years ago, and drilling from the bit had not punctured the block of coal.

In 1834, a little hammer with its cross section being only one inch in diameter was found in London, Texas encased in stone that was estimated to be one hundred million years old. It has not rusted since being found and its wooden handle has turned into coal. Most mining hammers of the eighteen hundreds would be much larger.

Workers in a stone quarry in France during the eighteen hundreds came across tools embedded in a layer of limestone fifty feet underground. T.D. Porter recorded the find in the American Journal of Science and Arts in 1820. The wood of the instruments had turned into agate.

In 1961, three people were out searching for geodes for a gift shop when they found one that had what looked like a spark plug inside it. The geode was dated as being 500,000 years old. I've seen a copy of the X-ray of the geode, and the object doesn't look like a spark plug to me, but whatever it is, it's man-made.

In an ancient Egyptian quarry, huge walls exist that look like they were milled from some giant machine. I have a machine shop in my building. As I look at these granite walls, they look exactly like a huge cutter made these indentations, just like a mill cutter would make in the side of an aluminum block in my milling machine. Of course, the difference is that the granite walls these cuts have been made in are ten to fifteen feet high and two to three feet deep—but are perfectly cut with perfectly square inside corners! I know most people can't relate to this sort of precision, but if you're a machinist or an engineer, you've got to take your hat off to this sort of evidence.

What some researchers have discovered is that these perfectly cut granite blocks may have come from a much earlier civilization than the Egyptians. At the Khnum Temple Portico in Egypt, the popular belief is that its stones were quarried from the Ptolemaic period. This is because Alexander the Great's name is carved into the surface of one of the granite blocks. In that same quarry, precision-cut stones from a much earlier period are also found. Therefore, just because there is writing that can be dated on a stone, it does not necessarily date the carved stone's origin. The artifacts from a later culture are often inherited from a previous one, and they now have the privilege of putting anything they want on that property, where the previous culture may be erased forever.

Memories are short and legends of past generations that have endured to this day are few. History gets forgotten and often simply rewritten, where archeologists may be so proud as to believe their finding of every scrap of cuneiform as true. Many college students of our present generation have no idea who Boss Tweed was or that Dorothy Kilgallen may have been murdered because of her investigative reporting on the death of JFK. In fact, many will not associate the letters JFK with John Fitzgerald Kennedy. And most will have no idea why they called him, "Jack." Even modern history is often rewritten to suite the times. Japan has no record of the rape of Nanking in their school's history books. Germany had so many scholars wanting to rewrite historical events that they had to criminalize historical revisionism. Even in America, the planned systematic genocide of one and a half million Armenians was denied as ever having been considered. Currently Turkey and Azerbaijan deny that there was an Armenian genocide.

The entire experience of our planet, as far as aspects of our personal and interpersonal concepts of everything known, can be summed up as spanning no more about seventy years. Sure, technology has made advancements. Men of extraordinary wisdom have written down their take as to what makes us tick. But for those of humanity that forego reading about or learning from them, we remain mostly in the dark ages of available knowledge, fending for ourselves with our knowledge of the table scraps of history. We take our information about life for granted, learning from our surroundings and reacting according to that miniscule input. With only seventy years available to us, we are no more advanced in wisdom and understanding of our existence than any prior civilization—even those that have erased themselves off the face of the earth.

Those Fighting Youths

14

Teenagers' brains are actually not fully connected as they are later in life. Since the prefrontal cortex is where decisions are made, teenagers literally can't come to a decision as fast as they could in later life.

From the first grade through the senior years of school, fighting has always been a part of exhibiting prowess amongst peers. Studies show that violence on campus is on an upswing. When a fight broke out in my generation, we were sent to the principal's office for detention. In fact, fighting today has become so bad that in the past couple of decades, school violence has risen in such intensity and magnitude that students are now facing legal prosecution for their acts of violence. It's not just high school, either; middle school kids, ages from twelve to thirteen years, are being carted off by the police. When a policeman showed up in my school, he was revered and respected. He wasn't there to arrest someone; he was there to teach us about how to be careful when crossing the street and commending the school's patrol attendants that helped the younger students get off the school bus. This was in rural Ohio. When I got to California, things were very different.

Dr. Rashmi Shetgiri at the Los Angeles Biomedical Research Institute found that one in four teenage students had engaged in a fight during that school year. What he found is that Latino students were taught at home that fighting should be the last resort, while black parents expressed doubts on how effective alternate strategies really are. He did not interview the parents of whites.

In my research on fighting and youths, by chance I ran across a site under the heading "answers" that basically added fuel to many of my questions about fighting and the present generation. Here are some excerpts:

1. *I like fighting. I want to get into a street fight just because I think it would be fun. I enjoy being punched and kicked, but I like punching other people even more. I'm always punching or kicking something. I am always thinking about beating someone up. I punch my brother just for fun.*

2. *My family thinks I'm crazy. I just like fighting.*

3. *Fighting there gets really intense with lots of kicking and elbowing! And when you go against someone you feel the rush! Wooow!*

4. *I've met guys who fight because it's all they want to do. These guys thoroughly enjoy inflicting pain.*

5. *Martial arts has taught me a lot of self control, but last week, I've had this urge to fight the next kid that opens their mouth. This feeling just won't go away.*

I believe most guys have, at one time or another, had a penchant for the classic bar brawl. I remember an incident at Bell High School in California, which I attended beginning in the seventh grade through the first half of the tenth grade, where some guys were talking about a brawl they engaged in. They said it was really fun. A few guys got hurt, but mostly fists were flailing in the wind with few real connections. The excitement of the story strangely made me wish I had been there myself. This fascination with brutality may explain why young people develop a penchant for fighting.

Researchers know that many animals are drawn to fights. Here again is a study that supports the reward pathway in the brain that becomes engaged when responding to aggressive events. And again, dopamine is involved in the reward. What this study has further learned is that the same clusters of brain cells involved in rewards are also connected to a craving for violence. In a study that supports others where winning a fight involves dopamine, it was not conducted with humans but with mice.

What they did was place a male mouse in a cage with a female mouse where the male became accustomed to his surroundings. They then removed the female and let another male in. Signs of aggression soon resulted, and then, fighting and biting. After the bout of biting ended, the visiting mouse was removed from the ring. The resident mouse had been trained to poke a target with his nose to indicate that he wanted the intruder mouse to return for another match. What they found was that the resident mouse consistently poked the invitation target and consistently fought with his opponent over and over again.

The conclusion was that an individual will seek out aggressive encounters just because they experienced some rewarding sensation from it. They went further to test their hypotheses. The home mouse was treated with a drug that blocks the dopamine in the part of the brain that was known to be involved with rewards. Afterward, the treated mouse was less likely to request a rematch. This was proof for the first time that dopamine plays a critical role as a motivator for aggression.

Their conclusions also point to human implications, as the reward pathways in mouse brains are very similar to humans. They state that, "Almost all mammals are aggressive in some way or another." But is aggression in human society in any way beneficial?

That's a question that can have many skews. According to Austrian ethologist Konrad Lorenz, aggression is a necessary aspect of human nature. He was of the belief that aggression builds up in our bodies like fluid filling a tank, where at some point it overflows and needs to be released. This may be supported by the fact that more humans have been killed by members of their own species than any other animal.

In contrast to cows and sea turtles, hyenas appear to be genetically programmed for aggression. Even before their eyes are open, they have been seen to bite their siblings with their sharp little canine teeth.

In the animal kingdom, aggression is gauged by benefits over loss. This can also be a genetic trait in humans, where benefits in an aggressive act are justified. This is when the benefits are high and the costs are low. If two individuals, or even nations, for instance, have a desire or need for the same thing, and neither is willing to compromise or make a deal, then aggression can result. If the issue is survival, such as the need for food, then the price for aggression may not outweigh the cost. But for many humans, aggression is available at a very low cost. For example, an elderly woman is walking to her Mercedes in a mall parking lot. Her purse is draped over her shoulder and she's carrying a large bag of items she's just purchased. A street thug sees her and decides to make a grab for her purse. It's easily snatched and he quickly runs off to the safety of the darkened night. In this case, the cost is low and the act of aggression was of benefit to the thug.

In the case of aggression for survival for food, aggression may be beneficial to society. In the case of the thug, the benefit was only personal—society in general was in a small way damaged. If left without laws, aggression would turn into anarchy. Outside Los Angeles schools, in which one in four students surveyed had gotten into a fight on campus, a national survey found more disturbing statistics—their survey found one in three students had gotten into a physical fight during that year, which included those not on school property. Teachers today view fighting very differently than in the fifties when I went to school. Their take is that it's so common that it's just a part of growing up. The average age of a public school teacher in the US is 42.5—they could call me Papa. This means that in 1955, they would have been -19.5 (that's minus nineteen and a half years old). These teachers literally grew up in the new era of school fighting and never knew the existence of the tranquil, respectful and learning environment I went through.

I'm not comparing for the sake of saying it was better then than it is now. Every generation needs to make their mark, and this one today only appears to be more violent because they appear to be engaging in more fighting. If one watches recent movies of public school activities, I think they portray students as best they can. And, if that's what it's like, it's pretty damn different. They also appear to be less respectful of their teachers and elders. From the feedback I got from some of my teachers, I might fit in better in today's schools because of my propensity for questioning my teacher's veracity. A difference might be that I was not aggressive.

In that national survey, junior and senior high school students were asked to list what caused the fights they witnessed. They were:

1. Someone insulted someone else or treated them disrespectfully (54%).

2. There was an ongoing feud or disagreement (44%).

3. Someone was hit, pushed, shoved, or bumped (42%).

4. Someone spread rumors or said things about someone else (40%).

5. Someone could not control his or her anger (39%).

6. Other people were watching or encouraging the fight (34%).

7. Someone who likes to fight a lot was involved (26%).

8. Someone didn't want to look like a loser (21%).

9. There was an argument over a boyfriend or girlfriend (19%).

10. Someone wanted to keep a reputation or get a name (17%)

A couple of clinical psychologists weighed in as to why teenagers rebel and fight. Their conclusion was that their brains are developing, and as they develop, their judgment centers are learning about how their parents dress funny, that they are so out of touch. They see the world more realistically and construct ideal parents based on their friends' parents, which leads the belief that their parents are embarrassing. Good lord! General statements like this only make me think that only friends' parents are cool and mine aren't. There's got to be a better reason as to why teenagers are more prone to flexing their spirited self aggrandizement.

Again, in my opinion, these psychologists were close, but no cigar. It is in fact brain development, but for a very different reason than learning how their parents dress funny and that they are embarrassing. It has to do with the prefrontal cortex again. Yes, teenagers appear to take stupid risks, but they do because they think about them longer than adults. Counterintuitive? Let's look at this prefrontal cortex a bit closer.

Teenagers' brains are actually not fully connected as they are later in life. Since the prefrontal cortex is where decisions are made, teenagers literally can't come to a decision as fast as they could in later life. It's like the urge to eat that luscious piece of chocolate cake that comes quickly, and you're moving your hands toward it, but then you remember that you are on a health binge and mull over whether to eat it or not. Teens take an average of 170 milliseconds longer to review the consequences of whether the risk is worth the reward. By that time, they may have already eaten the cake—just kidding of course. The result from this study is that they are more prone to taking risk than adults. It's the amygdala/prefrontal cortex dialogue with the hypothalamus, which works in conjunction along with other centers, that makes it all happen. In any case, teenagers are more prone to taking risk because of an underdeveloped prefrontal cortex as we continue.

In another study using MRI scans, it was discovered that teenagers' brains reacted very differently from adults in the presence of friends when faced with a decision. They found that teens that were not prone to take risk were much more apt to take the same risk in the presence of their friends. The reward centers became much more active when friends were watching. In college students and adults, this level remained constant no matter who was watching.

These studies revealed that teen brains are more childlike in their development. Their bodies may appear to be maturing, but their brains remain as they did when they were younger and more apt to throw temper tantrums. When teenagers were assigned a task, they found a large amount of activity in their underdeveloped prefrontal cortex than they did in adults. This meant that their brains were trying to absorb and process everything they could, resulting in a literal overload of their little prefrontal cortex. This can lead to frustration and short tempers. The adult brain works much more efficiently, which makes concentrating on a single thing much less complicated.

On top of that, it was found that teenagers have a much harder time correctly interpreting vocal inflections and facial expressions and will react irrationally to emotional situations. A photo of a person with a specific expression was shown to teenagers and adults. Every adult described the expression as fear while the majority of the teenagers said they saw anger and even shock. This experiment showed that teenagers and adults used two completely different parts of their brains during the MRI scan when viewing the photo. The teenagers used the part of the brain that controls emotions, while adults used the part that controls logic and reason.

The conclusion was that the teenager's brain has a much greater chance of misinterpreting an emotion. This is because that part of the brain that they use makes them more likely to react irrationally and over the top.

This could account for a teenager misinterpreting being "dissed," dwelling in a misinterpreted emotion and taking an aggressive action which results in confrontation, which results in a fight, which results in retaliation, and on and on. This is notwithstanding that males are filled with testosterone, piss and vinegar. For those teenagers reading this, "piss and vinegar" is an old expression used by novelist John Steinbeck in his novel *In Dubious Battle* in 1936. "Listen, mister", London said, "them guys is so full of piss and vinegar they'll skin you if you show that slick suit outside." With those vibrant physical bodies, their belief in invincibility, high levels of anti-fear hormones, a little weak prefrontal cortex with a lowered level of logic; what in the world can we expect but that this species within our species will relish the engagement and excitement of the inevitable fight?

We Come Here By Design

15

This field is called behavioral genetics. These studies say that personality traits are polygenic. This means that there are multiple genes involved in any personality trait.

Every living thing came into this physical Universe like a wrapped present. There's something inside each and every one of these containers that ranges from strange to wonderful, beautiful to ugly, passive to aggressive. Whether we like it or not, we are all pre-contained. The color of our eyes, the shape of our heads, the size of our nuts (if we happen to be a pecan tree) are all pre-encoded within the protein-producing DNA that comprises all living things. A chameleon cannot fly and a rose bush cannot run away from a florist. Good thing I didn't say a tree cannot bark; that might have been misleading. We are what we are and can't be anything but. I've actually tried to be totally serious about things, but those humor genes always seem to work themselves into my thoughts. If I were a scorpion, I'd probably laugh every time I stung something. I just can't help being me, and that's my point in this chapter.

Genetics began with the work of Augustinian friar Gregor Johann Mendel when he worked with pea plants. In 1866, he published what came to be known as the Mendelian inheritance. This led to many studies, especially on the fruit fly because of its fast generative reproduction. This led to investigations of the physical nature of the gene in the fifties, where experiments showed that DNA was the portion of chromosomes that contained genes. By the seventies, scientists were manipulating genes through genetic engineering and sequencing entire genomes. In 1977, DNA was sequenced for the first time, and in 2003 the successful completion of the Human Genome Project, where it was sequenced to 99% with 99.99% accuracy, occurred. In 2016 a genome was sequenced in outer space.

DNA is the program that runs living organisms. It's the code that's embedded within life that determines the shape and structure of something that has the magical ability so that it's able to perceive its surrounding environment. Photons from a nearby star, our sun, are perceived by living entities as warmth. Molecules of two parts hydrogen and one part oxygen are felt as wetness. The earthworm perceives dirt and animal manure as food. There's more magic in DNA than all the illusionists the world has ever seen, and yet we are totally oblivious to its mysterious origin.

We know that RNA most likely predated DNA, and RNA has been created in laboratories. Latest studies indicate that DNA might have evolved as a storage polymer and became genetic material after RNA. In other words, DNA could have been a two-step process. They have also learned that extremophile microbes could have survived in space and seeded many planets, opening up the possibility that life is abundant in the Universe. If you've read my previous books, you'll know my stance on this one. I don't *believe* extraterrestrials have visited us, I *know* they have. If there weren't so many books on the subject, I'd write my version of the sightings I've had and the personal eyewitnesses I've interviewed who have seen alien beings—up front and personally! But, I digress. Back to DNA…

We believe we've decoded the genome (99%), the near complete set of DNA, and yet the noncoding DNA, that which does not encode protein sequences, are referred to as junk. What is it that we don't know about junk DNA?

I've been under the unsubstantiated belief that all this junk DNA somehow has to do with our seat of desire, the mind—the id. Others are studying DNA for answers to personality traits. I believe that in order for us to be experience-driven beings, the motivation for quests in life must be encoded into some physical part of our brains like the physiology of what makes schizophrenics, psychopaths and just plain mean people who they are. It's also what makes Grandma so sweet and what brings joy from a loving mate. But, since this book is about why people fight, I'll stay the course.

Bad guys' brains react differently to certain stimuli than the neurotypicals, and this is a physical manifestation, not just a nonphysical psychological mystery. Brain scans are showing the actual regions that light up when people go from normal to angry or into a state of euphoric lovemaking. Something is encoding our neurological system to get the brain to do these things that we can actually see on little TV screens based on some external stimuli. So far the consensus is that DNA makes proteins, and I've found very little about it making personality—maybe through proteins in the brain, but personality nonetheless.

Much work has been done to compare the personalities of fraternal twins that share about 50% of their genes to those of identical twins who share 100% of their genes. The clearest evidence of genes having an influence over personality was done by Jang, et al, in 1996. They found that fraternal twins shared 23% of personality traits while identical twins shared 46%. But which genes account for the similarities? One study that has been ongoing for the past fifteen years is specifically looking for small repeating sections of genes; namely, single nucleotide polymorphism, which has identified a version of a specific gene. One breakthrough of the study is the ApoE4 genetic polymorphism linked to Alzheimer's disease. So far the personality gene remains elusive, and the prevailing evidence suggests that there are no personality genes.

But is this correct? What about the identical twins with such similar personalities? What other factor but genetics could be responsible for this? Some researchers are under the belief that we are missing something. Jamie Derringer pushed for research in single nucleotide polymorphism and sensation-seeking behavior. What was different about Jamie's work was that it didn't rely on association of a single nucleotide polymorphism, but how they relate to dopamine and how they relate in concert to express a personality trait. The findings of this research were at least promising.

As Dr. Michael Kraus explains, "One possible answer arises from understanding what happens to DNA before it is expressed as a personality characteristic." He goes on to say, "In short, genes need to be expressed at a cellular level in order to influence personality, and so one place where a genetic researcher might want to look to examine gene influences on personality is at this expression—that is, what genes are being unzipped by RNA, so that specific hormones/proteins are produced?"

More recently a new field of scientific study has emerged to dedicate its work to understanding the genetic components of personality. This field is called behavioral genetics. These studies say that personality traits are polygenic; this means that there are multiple genes involved in any personality trait. In addition, there are environmental influences to contend with. It's a complex process because of how both genetics and environment interact in the formation of personality. In order to find a specific personality gene, one would have to isolate a specific personality trait and tie it to a specific gene. The difficulty would be like taking several paint colors out of their cans, mixing them together, and then taking them back apart and returning them back into their cans in their original colors. It gets even more complex when some of these paints are made of different pigments, such as found in lacquer, enamel and power coat.

Due to this complexity, researchers have taken sort of a backdoor approach in their methods, using the twin studies, family studies and adoption studies. Twin studies will indicate behavioral differences between fraternal and identical twins. Family studies are used to determine if certain traits run in families and compare the 50% of the genes that they share with each of their parents. The adoption studies compare similarities between adopted parents and biological parents. Although these studies cannot isolate genes relating to any specific trait, it will demonstrate the influence of the collective genes with specific traits that show commonality.

A study of twins was conducted from Edinburgh University in Scotland that indicated that we are more genetically predisposed with personality than we are environmentally. They studied more than 800 sets of identical twins and non-identical twins to determine whether it was upbringing or genetics that had a greater effect on their drive for success. They were able to derive personality traits from well-established psychological scales. This study was lead by Professor Timothy Bates, who said, "Previously, the role of family and the environment around the home often dominated people's ideas about what affected psychological wellbeing. However, this work highlights a much more powerful influence from genetics." He goes on to say, "If you think of things that people are born with, you think of social status or virtuoso talent, but this is looking at what we do with what we've got.

"The biggest factor we found was self control. There was a big genetic difference in [people's ability to] restrain themselves and persist with things when they got difficult and react to challenges in a positive way."

This study reminds me of a very successful businessman that once said, "Some people are not successful because they just don't have the genetic material." This was long before the genome project, but it made sense even back in the sixties when I heard it. What does this say about people with a propensity to fight over a disagreement rather than methodically look for solutions? Would these people prefer confrontation in hopes that their adrenaline-starved bodies, regulated by brain proteins and circuits, be satisfied by the sheer act of winning? Is the urge to fight because their parents were abusive, or is it because their parents contained a certain combination of genetic material? Was it because they were abusive from genes attained from Grandma and Grandpa and inadvertently passed these on to their offspring? Should we continue to learn about our gene pool in order to identify and correct defective genetic personality traits or should we just live with the pain? I think the idea of living with the pain might not be a bad one. After all, we are also endowed with free will and choice. Not all abused children grow up to be monsters and not all monsters were abused.

Quelling down the monster title, let's discuss building character through learning from pain. My mom used to make me wash the dishes after every meal. I hated it. I would stand there, pouting and working as slowly as I could so that she might give up on me because it took so long. She never did. She was building character, a subconscious work ethic that stemmed also from mowing the lawn with a push-mower, raking the leaves in the front yard and cleaning my room. Fortunately, I was not genetically predisposed to retaliate against authority, but I still hated when it interfered with my playtime. Over time, I learned that if I did the dishes really quickly, I had more time for play, and if I pushed that old-time lawn mower faster, it became fun watching the grass flying off the blades. It worked its way into a challenge rather than a chore. The same worked for shoveling the snow from the driveway and the walkway to our front step.

What I was not aware of was that my mom, in her wisdom, was building my work ethic through repetition. Where she learned this, I don't know, but the previous generation appeared to just know these things without the Internet, Facebook or YouTube. Character building can be the result of many activities, such as parenting, civil debating, problem solving, managing and dealing with people, of course, hard work, and last but not least, conflict. Conflict doesn't necessarily mean fighting, but fighting and putting a bully of sorts back in his place can in fact build character. And, not only for the winner of the fight, as was the case with one fight I was in where the attacker, the bully, lost the fight and showed up at my house after he came back from the hospital that night to shake my hand.

Based on some of these studies, the tide may be shifting more toward us being genetically predisposed than environmentally influenced, although both play vital roles. Genetic influences run in a deeper vein, such as the innate drive to succeed and a capacity to love. Genetics may also be responsible for the antagonist within acting against the protagonist traits that encourage aspects of goodness within our psyche. This may be the good vs. evil that's inside us. It's the actions we take that mold our character and can overshadow our negative genetic propensities. Our decisions over what we do with pain, whether it's physical or psychological, builds upon previous experiences to form our character. Our genetics are our foundation by design. By further experiences and decisions, we modify and mold our initial foundation. Without pain, there would be no building. Without pain, there would be no reference to good. Without pain, there would be no spiritual growth.

16

Two Realities

Physical reality seems to be consistently attacking mental reality by its unbreakable rules we must comply with.

As I see it, there are basically two realities that we have to contend with. One is the mental reality and the other is the physical part that our mental perceptions and beliefs have to contend with. I was putting on my pants this morning and one leg went right in, but the other one got stuck right at the final stitched end. This gave my toes just enough resistance that I lost a bit of balance, since I was holding myself up with only one leg. I was like a flamingo that was off balance. Why do flamingos stand on one leg? Because if they lift it up, they would fall down like I almost did, right? It wasn't earth-shaking; in fact, it's happened many times, but it still annoys me a bit when it does. Of course, it's a miniscule event, but my mental reality was that if one leg went through, the other one should do the same, *and it didn't*.

These two realities, the mental one and the physical one, are often in conflict. For example, let's say we're in California driving around a curve we take every day going to work. Our experience is that we usually go around that turn at thirty-five miles per hour, but today it's raining, so we decide to go around the curve at twenty-five miles per hour. The car loses traction and we slide off into the guardrail. The water had loosened the oil that was embedded in the asphalt and it was much slipperier than we thought. Our car is dented where it hit the guardrail and we are absolutely pissed. Different people will react differently and the psychopath may even get out and punch the guardrail and break a few phalanges (bones of the hand).

It can get much worse than this, and of course, when it does, we can get much angrier.

Anger can be the result of physical reality not complying with our mental reality of how things should be. What has to be understood is that physical reality takes precedence. We'd like to believe that our new sports car with the best tires money can buy could go around that same curve on a nice sunny day at sixty miles per hour. If it doesn't make it, some of us will blame the sun, the tires, the suspension or anything that comes to mind. Some people will blame themselves, while others will go home and kick the family cat. The reality of it is that physical reality always wins over the mental reality of a preconceived outcome. That's usually when reality sets in.

We often get conflicted with physical reality. Our mental views create expectations, and when those expectations are not met, we begin to lean toward a disturbed mental state. This may be temporary, or it may grow into a neurosis or even into some form of psychosis. Mental health is not taught in schools as a subject like physical education and general bodily health. When we think of mental health, we think of crazy people seeing psychologists or psychiatrists in order to fix some delusion or repair a relationship between opposing personalities, maybe even between two crazy people. Often it's parents bringing their uncontrollable teenagers in for therapy or a wife bringing her husband in to get him fixed (his brain, not his testicles—that's a different sort of doctor).

In any case, I learned the idea below a long time ago and it's served me very well. It's not what it first appears to be, and it may be a little hard to get your head around, but it works to maintain a level of personal peace, especially in the face of some challenge one may face.

What's healthy for our psychological being is that we remain responsible for every decision we make. What I mean by this is that if something goes awry, blaming anything, even ourselves, is not a healthy point of view for our psyche. But, it's not as simple as that. Many people have said this. Let's look at it from a perspective that there are two of you living inside your brain. One is the person that has to deal with all the challenges of life. The "other you" is an observer that's literally disconnected from all your perils. It's like your neighbor looking at you and laughing as you trip over your porch step and fall on your face. You're upset and ready to kill the contractor that made the step and your neighbor is laughing his ass off. The difference is in the semantics of the words "blame" and "responsibility."

Living in the "blame" part of your psyche is where most people reside. Since we are always right with the decisions we make, it's only natural that anything that happens to us that we don't like is the fault of someone or something else. The klutz that's always bumbling around with low kinesthetic talent may say, "I just slipped on a wet floor in this supermarket; who can I sue?"

This person, the blame us, gets annoyed, upset, angry and is even motivated to take some sort of physical action against any perpetrator or any action that brought that person to the point of victimhood and blame. This person may even be motivated to punch a guardrail—it was all that damned guardrail's fault. The blame part of us often amplifies this act into escalated warfare, whether it's actually physical or just a mental scenario of retaliation. Since thoughts are things, the subconscious views these as real and if we do this enough times, we slowly develop into just an angry person with a bottom lip always poking out. It's been said that people with this sort of lip will eventually drown when it rains.

The responsible part of us is that part that takes responsibility over everything that occurs. Very few people live in that "us." I believe most of us live somewhere in between. There's a lot of information about taking responsibility, but being responsible for things that you have been a victim of is a different perspective. Let's say you are walking down the street and a car goes out of control and hits you. Both your legs are broken and you are in lots of pain. You are in the hospital for surgery to have pins put in your leg bones and are out of work for months. There's a problem with your insurance and your monetary compensation is delayed and you fall behind on your house payments and the bank has no mercy on you. In such a case, were you responsible? In a court of law, the driver is responsible for your misery. For most people, the blame shifts to the idiot whose car he made to go out of control. He's responsible for all damages, and rightfully so, by law.

It would seem only natural to ask yourself, "Why me?" What if you, in this case, were to say to yourself, "Well, I made the decision to be on the sidewalk at that time; therefore, I am just as responsible as the driver that hit me." For most rational thinking people, that would make no sense whatsoever. You weren't doing anything wrong when this moron decided to do something stupid that made his car go out of control. There's a major difference in living in the blame self rather than living in the responsible self, and that's a line that I once heard from a popular motivational speaker. It's been used by many psychologists ever since, and that's "the subconscious can't take a joke." This is because it's merely a storage bin that takes everything literally. If you think garbage thoughts, then it eventually becomes a garbage bin. The bad part about this is that your subconscious is where we regurgitate our decisions from—garbage in, garbage out.

I don't suggest that you become a target for negativity by simply accepting every injury that comes your way and saying, "Well, it's my fault for even being born." There's a huge difference between portraying yourself as a victim and being responsible for the Universe around you. It's the input to your inner self, the subconscious that makes the difference. Because if a car that went out of control (figuratively) hit you, it would be easy, even downright lazy to accept the victim role that shit happened and it was their entire fault—even though it in fact was. What would you be feeding that part of your brain that can't take a joke? The data entered would be that of victimization. The feedback from the subconscious would be that victims have no control over the outcome of an event that came from an outside source. Taking responsibility for being in the wrong place at that time feeds your subconscious with the data that you are in control of any and all events. With that, the decision to take positive actions to the best of your creative powers keeps your reality of thought in a much healthier mental space.

I was listening to the radio this morning and a woman called in to get legal advice to sue a veterinarian because her dog had died of cancer after he removed a tumor from the dog. A second veterinarian told her that if they would have brought the dog in earlier, they could have done something. The woman wants to sue the first vet for not doing that "something." The second vet never said what that "something" was, but the woman was so distraught over the loss of her dog that she wanted to blame someone for *not* doing that "something" that she believed caused her dog's death. However, if one looks at this globally and asks, could it have been "something" in the dog's diet that she fed him that caused the cancer? What if she could not afford the thousands of dollars she claimed she spent on his treatment, would the dog have died anyway? Aren't veterinarians compassionate people that do their best? In my humble opinion, blaming someone for doing his or her best isn't part of my internal constitution.

For this woman, physical reality overshadowed her post mental perception of what should have happened rather than what did happen. Her anger is the product of her action of taking the dog to a second vet. There could be many reasons for this woman being angry enough to sue the first vet. Here are just a few:

1. The second vet has a huge ego and feels he can cure cancer, but the patient needs to be brought in earlier.

2. The second vet knows the first vet that took some of his business away and he just wants to badmouth him as part of an ongoing vengeance routine.

3. The second vet was so compassionate and caring at this woman's pain that he wanted to console her rather than saying, "There's nothing we can do."

4. The second vet saw that this woman had money, treated the dog, and it died anyway.

5. The first vet really knew what he was doing.

Physical reality seems to be consistently attacking mental reality by its unbreakable rules we must comply with. This is like putting on your pants and going off-balance because the physical part of your toes hanging up at the cuff just didn't comply with what you mentally had planned. Physical reality is rigid, unbending, while our mental reality is fluid, dynamic, shapeable and worst of all, prone to fancy. The challenge is that there is only one physical reality, while each and every one of us resides in a completely different mental one. In addition to that, we even have thousands, maybe even millions of mental scenarios that the physics of life seem to be attacking. Golfers are hit by lightening, shoppers continue to slip on wet floors, a bird once pooped on my head—all of which are physical experiences that took our mental experience of the day by surprise. When we fight, we use the rules of physical reality to mete out our own displeasure where physical reality really doesn't care if we knock each other's brains out. Here's where our subconscious is intrinsically linked with physical reality—the subconscious really doesn't care either!

It's well accepted that the subconscious records within its library everything that we've experienced in life. Psychologists have come to that conclusion from reports of people such as World War II pilots that survived being shot down and their entire lives flashed before them before hitting the ground or the water. This may have to do with the shock of their belief that this was the end—that they were in fact going to die.

Our subconscious, that data collection center, may be attached to some uploading mechanism after our death. In fact, it may be all that's needed for people to have a life's review during a traumatic event or a near-death experience. Sir Roger Penrose of Cambridge University and Sam Parnia of Stony Brook University School of Medicine suggest that this data is uploaded into the quantum realm at death and this is the data that's in our subconscious storehouse. If this is the case, then the data portion in the brain's recording device is what we measure ourselves against as to whether we were naughty or nice during that review. From the eight million Americans that have had a near-death experience, the consensus is that we are not judged, but rather we judge ourselves—and that could be the hardest judgment we could muster.

We use laws of the physical Universe in order to inflict physical pain on others, which can also result in mental pain. The receiver of that pain cannot negate the effects of a blow to the head or the pain of a bullet piercing the flesh. The instigator of that act feels nothing, and should that person be even a bit psychopathic, they will feel no empathy. Even when ultimate fighters engage in a bout for sport, after they have literally knocked the opponent out and he has fallen to the canvas, they are often seen delivering additional blows to the head or face of the limp, out-cold dude (and even dudettes do this). The rush of conquest can trigger the euphoric state to continue punishment in an adrenaline-induced state of exhilaration. All this is recorded and somehow uploaded in that life's review. All of which will become felt, not just from the vantage of the one having the review, but from the experiences of every other person that was affected by that person's actions. The person responsible for mass killings will experience every pain felt by their victims, their victims' loved ones and their friends. It's the most fair form or restitution ever imagined.

I can attest to the fact that the mental reality has far more depth and impact than this physical one. I've been out of my body three times and experienced the strength and magnitude of what it's like being alive in a thought world. I can't even imagine what it would be like to experience the pain and suffering of someone like Dr. Josef Mengele, who sent so many to the die in the gas chambers of Auschwitz, did at his life's review. When a mother asked Mengele where her baby was, she was told not to worry; that she would see her baby soon. She later asked again and Mengele told her to look at the camp's smokestacks. My hat off to whoever came up with the idea of a life's review and its self-inflicting effects.

Fighting happens. I can never say that I'm correct in my ideas because I haven't been on the planet long enough to collect all the data on life and what the plan might be for life in its fundamental form. I've read too many books and other writings that make such claims that appear to have answers to everything, from levels of heaven to "God is irrelevant." As I mentioned, our life span is short. We simply cannot collect the wisdom of our history within one lifetime; therefore, collectively, the entire human race is only about seventy years old with only seventy years of experience. Studies show that aggression starts around two years old and crime rises in the early teens. There was very little information available on anger throughout life, but I did find a graph where the most discontent age with life on a happiness scale was right at fifty years old. The graph slowly rose to that state and then fairly quickly dropped off to pretty happy again around seventy. Of course, that's where I am …

I had a wonderful and enlightening phone conversation with the Coordinator of the San Diego IANDS, Beverly Brodsky. Beverly had a near-death experience after a motorcycle accident. During her sojourn into the spirit realm she was shown the wonders of the Universe. Beverly is a very intelligent and inquisitive person, and her questioning was what I might have asked had I been there. Merely being conscious out of your body is far different from an actual near-death experience. All her questions were answered about everything, from the creation's source to why we are here. Upon her return to her body, the enormity of information quickly vanished. All she could remember was that she *knew*, and now she can't recall those delicious details. I believe Beverly's simple answer to the mysteries and reasons for life's existence, the ups and downs, the love and the fighting has cleared many questions for me, although I have many more. When I asked her about her near-death experience, about the deeper mysteries of life and what she had learned, her beautiful answer was, "I don't think we are supposed to know."

www.ingramcontent.com/pod-product-compliance
Lightning Source LLC
Chambersburg PA
CBHW061741050726
47598CB00002B/559